Yellow Rain

Also by Mai Der Vang

Afterland

Yellow Rain

Poems

Mai Der Vang

Graywolf Press

This publication is made possible, in part, by the voters of Minnesota through a Minnesota State Arts Board Operating Support grant, thanks to a legislative appropriation from the arts and cultural heritage fund. Significant support has also been provided by Target Foundation, the McKnight Foundation, the Lannan Foundation, the Amazon Literary Partnership, and other generous contributions from foundations, corporations, and individuals. To these organizations and individuals we offer our heartfelt thanks.

This book is made possible through a partnership with the College of Saint Benedict, and honors the legacy of S. Mariella Gable, a distinguished teacher at the College. Support has been provided by the Manitou Fund as part of the Warner Reading Program.

Published by Graywolf Press
250 Third Avenue North, Suite 600
Minneapolis, Minnesota 55401

www.graywolfpress.org

Published in the United States of America

ISBN 978-1-64445-065-9

2 4 6 8 9 7 5 3 1
First Graywolf Printing, 2021

Library of Congress Control Number: 2020951357

Cover design: Jeenee Lee Design

Rau peb ib tsoom hais neeg Hmoob

Contents

Because as long as these words live you will not die. And if the acid of time and warlike tempests pull them down, you will not die. And we will not die again.

—Raúl Zurita, *INRI*

Yellow Rain

I have been following the rains, hunting them in my dreams.

Yellow rain. Biological warfare. The Hmong. Erasure of a people's history, negation of trauma. Shadows and truth.

First came the wars that led to other wars that led to the Secret War that became a proxy war in 1960s Laos, led by the Central Intelligence Agency. The white foreigner arrived bearing guns and bombs to lead his surrogate cause, to quell communism and use Hmong men to do his work of war. In breach of Laos' neutral state and a deepening of secrets.

1975. The war came crumbling down and all was lost to the communist victors of Vietnam and Laos. Almost everyone fled, deserting what was once home.

Yellow rain came in the midst of exodus, poison landed on the Hmong in the middle of escape. Specks descending from aircraft overhead, falling onto trees, into water, and onto skin. Specks of a mysterious substance ranging in color: red, black, white, green, and yellow above all. Specks of illness and death.

I am a daughter of Hmong refugees: mother and father were among the fled, which makes me among the fled. Second child and firstborn in a new land, daughter who keeps looking back at the sky.

Guide for the Channeling

Toward a worn legacy
of rain, I have been lost
down every jungle path,

adrift and senseless to
split open a cascade of
knowing. I have tried with

all my limber to keen a
credo of justice, shelter
those who solace inside

graves. I have been boiled
in my bladed search,
opening with questions

of a deserted pain to end
with a cemented breath
shattered into silk. This is

where I am taking you:
into a discarded vista
blowing forth a silent blaze.

Here in sunk villages
of the disregarded. Here
where even the dirt of

the land cannot muster
against the threat of air.
Biomedical, vegetation,

munitions unfound, every
footprint incarnate.
Where highlands tangle

their echoes to the ground.
A place no matter how
remote will always be

too near and too much
a reminder of an expired
war. Refugees not called

as people only to be
called the outcome of an
event. We are venturing

into swell beyond swelling
of paperwork and protocol,
slips of memo and routing,

cable and classified meeting.
Here is the talk: biological
weapon, yellow spots,

apiary blame, for decades
to wane and cold
filed. Believe me as a

torch of this wandering
that I have been digging
within the origins of

redaction. Believe where
I am sending you. I have
been shoveling upside

down. And now my eyes
stagger, my hands ache,
my legs becoming hunter,

my back a raging shadow.
I have been gardening myself
into this remembrance.

Declassified

May the dead   be ever-evidenced

    May their clandestine names
bellow from the mouth   of an August

  monsoon   May they coax the truth
        from every storm

  Long ago
     there lived a jungle
whose only cloth was   camouflage

All those who came to it
     learned the burden of hiding

       Long ago   we memorized
the refrains of wild birds

  stitched them underneath
     our evacuated skins

Then man   Then soldier Then vividness

    of saffron and canary
      arriving as small showers

    divulging its anatomy
      to the ecosystem

To keep the covert buried is not
how this story bends

  The insects have always known

Their lineage of pollen   and the children
                            of insects know too

May this Secret War   its author of poisons

    its professor of counterfeit treaties
kidnapper of honeybees   each iota

of its polluted doing

    may it all burn and blister
        under its own nakedness

The Fact of the Matter Is the Consequence of Ugly Deaths

> *It's not fair . . . to not consider . . . other stories . . . other frames of the*
> *story. . . . Ronald Reagan used this story to order the manufacture of*
> *chemical weapons . . . first time in twenty years. If the United States were*
> *to manufacture chemical weapons again . . . use them because the Russians*
> *supposedly had . . . people would have died ugly deaths in the consequence.*
>
> —**Robert Krulwich, Radiolab/WNYC, September 23, 2012**

Out here, it's parlors of jungle.

Sometimes flashbacks
    Of disfigured interrogations,

Handprints fleeing
To leave no crease
Behind.

        This is our monsoon
    To shelter, our version

    Of mortality snaking toward
            Delusional truth.

We know how to let go,
Then perish
With even more lineage of beauty.

        For thickening of truces
Between false men,

Aging purveyors of
    Genetically modified diplomatics.

        Lizard citizens invented.
    Herbicidal biomediation.

Whistling riddles
       Into an arsenal of hammers.

Spit of your unhinging.

       You refuse our dead,

As though
We were never alive.

Just say what you mean to say, that is:

       Hmong,
Keep
Your dying
To yourself.

Anthem for Taking Back

Even after   what shrivels

on pillows

are the syllables   of a dream

and our braided furies huddle

under porch light

After skyline of lashes

close over   our ocular machines

and a lightlessness governs

the way we move our arms

Long from now

how every breath   turns out

a copy of the air before and all air

moves through us   as cotton

What we heed

after a fluorescence capes

the skin   of our early moon

Whatever be the scourge

thumping inside our ears

Ember our wings

out of exile it says   ember loudly

all   of our furious tellings

They Think Our Killed Ones Cannot Speak to Us

As if to adjourn all
oxygen from the neck

is how they try to take
the voice   As if attempts

to render us pale   Ripped
lungless from woke into

wild ash   As if ashes
cannot blink howl testify

with the pulse of their own
tatters   As if hymn and

whistle   Hail and pour
We've seen how they

shame the light Stripped
hollow tearing out

filigrees of stars from
protocols of dust to make

drink a bouquet of venom
sprayed down a constellation's

throat   They must be so
earless as if we've no legs

to kneel   We are each
other's memory of the

future forty years from
here   Arriving at ourselves

by way of the dead
History will not beget

powder will not beget
myth will not make us

into marginalia   As ever
possessed by what we

have lost   There are no
language barriers in the

afterlife   A toxin is a
toxin is a toxin is the man

made truth is the dead who
leave everything behind

These bodies under the rains: vomiting, nausea, diarrhea, respiratory issues, chest pains, dizziness, blurred vision, blisters, and lesions. Cases of hemorrhaging and bloody diarrhea culminating in death.

I think of them not only battling an enemy but also battling their own bodies. Then the unknowable. The truth buried in the jungles. How do you elude the shape of something you cannot name?

Attacks came through the dry seasons and even at times during the wet, aimed primarily at remote areas like Phou Bia, a mountainous refuge for the Hmong resistance. In some cases, whole villages perished. The State Department reported more than 6,000 died from yellow rain. Some scholars and human rights organizations contend a larger number: possibly 20,000 to 40,000 Hmong casualties.

Fingers were pointed at and allegations denied by the Soviet Union charged with backing the communist governments of Vietnam and Laos.

Yellow rain had fallen before and would fall again, claims surfacing elsewhere: during the Yemeni civil war of 1963–67, against Khmer Rouge soldiers, attacks on mujahideen resistance fighters, Azerbaijan, Mozambique, the Iran-Iraq War. A substance with many aliases, places of historical use, potential origins, but stealth enough to never be rooted.

A Body Always Yours

It felt like a knife in the ribs

As if their body was going to blow up

The teeth to feel loose and the gums to smell rotten

Anyone whose bare skin was touched by a droplet to suffer severe necrosis of the affected area . . . died as a result of the "rotting" of their skin . . . took about two weeks to die

Native medicine was used to counter the effect was made from an infusion of sugar cane, a green-skinned pumpkin-like gourd and opium . . . carried in bamboo containers

—Cable, November 20, 1979; Report Questionnaire
Attachment, February 13, 1980

For what will be
    The chrome of your ribs

  A coronation faceted
To the bead of your bone's cameo

    For how you will asylum
  Your incisors into the clay

Of your jaws
For the terrarium of another day

You do not need to crumble
    You will not distort

From the shape
You've always been

    All pieces of you
    Together

As ever at birth
All pieces elixired   with sugarcane

Gourd
Tonic of opium   elixired

        From a call to grow arms
It will not take a severed meadow

To publish your ransacked gown
    Wrest apart   the sprouting

              Of an armory to mend
    This scarred biology

    You will not be   unheeded
If only   to banner   the truth

Gather now   your pigments
     And resist

        Endure
              Beyond   a fortnight

Ill of the Dubious

| Pork poisoned | appetite of contamination | poised for refugees to consume | in the nation next door for persons misplaced | Poisoned pork or pork contaminated was fed to Hmong refugees | in a camp for the campless in a place called Nong Khai | on day four on day five in the month of April in the year '79 | Hmong refugees ate the poisoned pork | from the bad hogs butchered in the abattoir | given them by camp workers | who all ate from the same hogs | where persons 3,000 who ate from the bad hogs were Hmong inside the camp of Nong Khai | At which vomit dealt to over 500 | At which alongside with diarrhea of severity | detriment to the vision | at which there was penchant for sleep | So children | total eight | adults | five of them | died | Eight children and five adult Hmong refugees died from eating poisoned pork fed to them in the camp at Nong Khai | while numerous at the camp who ate of the same but affected others were not | but affected were only Hmong | when poisoned pork was fed to Hmong refugees and some of them died | from bad hogs slaughtered on night before into 0800 hours meal of next day | Then two hours after | a man confessed of heavy head | muscle unrest | eyes to pop | dizzy with unable to sight | as others in the camp at Nong Khai ate the contamination | as soup with small pieces of pork had fewest effects | than ones who ate bad pork thrown into stir-fry | than most wildly poor outcome for refugees | who fed on entrees containing blood of bad hogs | In other cases | Hmong refugees given vegetables dusted in white powder | flavor of mysteriously unkind | As again | when powers in camp of Nong Khai fed poisoned cabbage with unknown bitter to Hmong refugees | but complain | and maybe just crave | but complain and was told | don't eat it then | but to shrivel | and thirst you | in your days as a person misplaced | in a camp for the landless | in a place where they stored you | served into fear | won't come your mouth to the spoon |

When the Poison Fell, Before 1979

I.

Hmong Refugee, Age 26, heard about attacks
March 1976, Ban Nong Khouy, 28 dead, red, green, and yellow smoke
September 1979, Ban Nam Kai, 27 dead

> You have followed
> How deep the ear-telling proceeds,
>
> Undensing these patterns
> To widen a vacancy of clues.
>
> To hear as you've heard
> Into the pulp's undergrowth.
>
> How much archiving
> Is too much sintered and fatigue?
>
> How digested the headlights
> Flare over the diseased hymn.

II.

Hmong Medic, Age 24, treated victims who experienced attacks
1976–1977, 49 villagers from Phu Chia

Last patient came to him in March 1977, all died within 24–48
hours, symptoms of red/swollen eyes, bitter taste in mouth,
convulsions, chest pain, difficulty breathing, darkened faces,
stiff necks, excessive flow of saliva

> Those who ended
> With you, toiled from hideouts
>
> Of crowded thorn,
> Crashed out of ridgeline only

To collide in a courtyard
Of exposure. Those who clawed

Along without fragrance
Of honey in their mouths, nor

Memory of stillness, nor
Enamel of face as an unchanged

Shade of Hmong. Those
Who wandered your way. Would

You have fed them
Remedy of ancestors or stray

Petitions arriving into
Gravity. What little you could

Bestow but a repairing
Face, triage of prayers.

III.
Hmong Refugee, Age 35, witnessed attack
September 1979, Ban Pha Lu

Bombs landed ten meters from him, gray and yellow smoke,
some of them did not go off (dark green artillery shell-like, dark
green cylindrical canister, unable to identify lettering because
he is illiterate); saw two people exposed who died within two
days, coughing up blood, runny noses, severe bloody diarrhea,
an additional twenty more people were killed in this attack;
he himself got sick: chest pain, cough, pain in eyes, stung like
hot peppers when he tried to breathe

Bring up your eyelids
To meet the horizon's climb,

Even as the carcinogen of a
Dire spice cauterizes you

To remember. An aching
Encounter with the fated two

Bound to the wild mist,
Where munitions occurred ten

Meters away, ten meters
From complicit artifacts awash in

A lettered truth, ten
Meters from crouching of proof.

IV.
Hmong Refugee, Age 56, experienced attack
Early 1978, Phu Chia

Two L-19 bombs were dropped on his village, red and black
smoke, six relatives died; he was told that he fell unconscious
for seven days within thirty minutes after attack; he felt bad
after regaining consciousness; fingernails and toenails were
black from hemorrhage, tongue stiff and could not talk for
seven days, lost vision for thirty days

How can a ceiling
Of translucence lift from a ground

So routinely sombered it
Has no Fahrenheit in which

To hibernate. The lemongrass
Might blade at first touch

But take a labor of calm
To salve your hands, feet giving

Back its truest blush.
Take that you lived and were

Offered the backbone
To tell, lessons on arriving at

The perimeter of a miracle.
They are yours to keep as this

Falling out of and back
Into have been yours to nestle,

Debris of the last epiphany
Ever yours to fulfill.

A Daub of Tree Swallows as Aerial Ash

> *Most serious charge, however, relates to report of massacre committed on May 15, 1985, in which "approximately 5,000 civilians were ordered into a cave at U.G. 332 820 and were 'gassed.'" These civilians reportedly were captured "at U.G. 332 803" on May 14, following a May 13 battle in which resistance fighters suffered heavy casualties at hands of Vietnamese and Pathet Lao soldiers. . . . Some twenty-five intended victims reportedly escaped being driven into cave. . . . Our efforts to date do not enable us to confirm any details of incident.*
> —**Cable from the US Embassy, Bangkok, to the Secretary of State, September 3, 1985**

All over threnodies
        of dissected   water

Inside this cavern of scars

Had the barn
owl been more accepting
                to tell

Had your sonatas petaled
        from below

                the walls of this
resounding abyss

Questioning what yielded
in your
        conduit of husk

        they cannot be sure of
details in preference

        to dismiss in fear
of the knives
sewn into
        their bones

They offer   no place
for you   but here is a place

        to rest your
                evening birdsong

Alongside
        a river of windows

        under a trellis of bells
to nourish

in silk leaves and a
        harvest of   wild pears

Case Studies in Escape, Post-1975

I. Hmong Village Chief

Five times your village was forced
To roam, restless and uprooted by

Eyes of the regime, to settle
    In the Ban Don Valley.

Wise ones taken to seminar
Meant this was a land of rules:

    No farming in the lowlands.
    No contact with the locals.
    No hunting within the forests.
    No trade outside the settlement.
    No clinics no schools.
    No elders allowed to spirit lead.

Monitored by
Two officials and a brigade.

    Then it happened,
    First attack in '79:

    Source saw a plane fly over and then
    saw "yellow sugar" on farm plants

Once more, December 1980.

Until no more withstanding:

    February 1981,
    Permission granted to move
    The village once more.

This time, you broke free:

      77 families to the Mekong.
      13 day walk.

II. Assistant to a "Red" Hmong Chief

    How many passages
        Did you offer to safety
  Before you conceded
          You could not
    Save the whole?

    You alongside the Gatekeeper
Who ended up on
        Your own side
  Of the war,
          Using his sway
  To free captives from
      Communist prisons.

The deep valley
      As the doorway
    He thrust open for all those
          Hmong on the move,
Hinting at foremost
        Route to pursue,
          Forfeiting
  His role as a red.

    Until the gas: 1978.

    No degree of begging
  To superiors came no
      Help for the ill.

    Second gas: June 1980.

Too small to treat
With opium were eight babies
          Thieved as a result.

Lost blood through body orifices.

Gatekeeper fled into
          The bush, seeking signal
                    If there is a plan to
                    Retake Laos.

  But there was no plan
  To balance what
                    You had been,

        No kindle
        Of a coup to shelter
                    All the hazards you gave.

III. Former Hmong Captain, Royal Lao Army

You averted your fate
In a cleansing camp.

            *People never
              Came back.*

If only you were
Quick as deer, atmospheric as bird,
Small as beetle to
          Hide in the earth.

Twenty-five relatives gone to the gas.

More had been forsaken
Without shield:

Eating roots and grass
For the last six months.

Children
And old people who can no longer
Walk are abandoned
In a cave

In the
Forest.

Fewer Hmong Are Dying Now Than in the Past

As though poaching
has absconded   As in
sufferers who thrive
while in captivity   Where has
the earmarked dying gone

May be partly due to the greater experience of the Hmong in dealing with yellow rain

Evolving toward loss
you are in a constant
mood of alter   pending
by the hour
to outlive the hypothesis
versus you

Treated themselves with opium after each attack

Still they
speculated   Clogging
their brains with
rival guesses

*Maybe H'Mong population had already been decimated by the high fatalities and refugee
exodus caused by earlier attacks dating back at least to 1976*

Do not stop
to bury the
slain

Suggests less lethal chemical agents or lower concentrations

Do not pause
to census the
ones extinct

Maybe H'Mong survivors were not taking time to count victims

For what matters
why you document   For whom
does tracking
give a means

Maybe surviving H'Mong people remaining in Laos were more wary and quick to take cover

If you are to hide and
flee in the wild   Grow out a new
existence in the name
of conservation

If this means the loss of your statistic

*Large force of Vietnamese after them that they had no chance to study the effect of the CW
agent on the plants*

Do not stop to
archive the foliage
There is no time   no mind
to make science
from your running

Signal for the Way Out

*When we left the village on the 14th of January I heard the funeral drums
and pipe—I don't know how many had died or if it was because of the chemi.*
—**CBW Questionnaire, March 7, 1984**

Onward in swells

Of supernal sleep   Onward these
        Rippling acoustics offered by

            A conjurer of the drum

You who fell back
        Be regaled and soul-throned

        By a minister of the reed

        Keeper of deathbeats
Waiting to be ceremonied out
                The ear

            This one is yours to womb

        This your audio of alpenglow
Precise to now leaving as deeply hued

            As the croon
            To resound
When land you finally reach

Self-Portrait Together as CBW Questionnaire

So Long As_____

We: Depart _____ from_____ the Middle _____

Of Our Embroidered Fairytale _____

So Long As in the Banishing _____

We Rescue a Hundred Whispers

Force the _____   Utterances _____

Of Our Feet _____   To Survive _____

Savor _____

The Warmth _____   We: Have Been _____ Vowed _____ You _____

At   The   _____ Region _____ Of _____

My Half: Untangling How Long _____

These Sterling Cords Combine _____

I See You Floating in a _____

Grid of Glitter _____

I TOUCH

_____ You Scaling Toward _____

_____ An Emerald Notion of Divine _____

_____ Waking Me to Inhale _____

_____ Ahead of This Breath _____

I Vivify _____

	SEND MY	CALFPRINT'S	WAFT
To Meet	_____	_____	_____
	_____	_____	_____
The Vocal	_____	_____	_____
	_____	_____	_____
	_____	_____	_____
	_____	_____	_____

Offering _____

Of Your Glove   _____

I Love You Even More in This War   _____

When (They Ask) _____

Why _____ Did _____   We _____   Live? _____

When They _____ Ask

What Kept _____ Our Force Forward?

Why Was _____ Death _____ Not Our Circumstance?

Are You Members   _____ Of

                                      _____ The

                                      _____ Resistance?

                                      _____ How

Many Days Walk

From Our First: _____ Name/ _____ To The/ _____ Airburst

Of Our Symptoms?

(We Answer) _____

Without: _____ Each _____ Other But _____ In _____ Phonetics

Of the Separate: Self _____ In Oneness _____ Of _____
Ourselves (Attained) _____:_____ With One

Another _____

____ You	_____ As the	_____
____ Blueprint	_____ Of My	_____
____ Atavistic	_____ Days	_____

Midnight of My Conscience

To Mirror _____   Your: Skin ____   Once ____   More ____   Frail ____

My   _____   Face   _____   Into   _____
The   _____   Lamp   _____   Of   _____

Your   _____   Eyes   _____   As   _____
If   _____   To   _____   See   _____

Out of Them

From Inside _____

_____

_____

Composition 1

Continue to grow along with the number of leaking chemical weapons

Costly to store and guard. Potential safety and physical security hazards.

The U.S. government received a report of an attack in March 1976 in the Ban Nong Khouy area. An unidentified aircraft released a red, yellow, and green substance that killed 28 people.

The U.S. government received a report of an attack in January 1977 in the Tam Lo area where an L-19 aircraft released a red substance. Source's father died about 12 hours after exposure while his mother died within 16 hours. The rest of his family died the following night.

The U.S. government received a report of an attack in March 1977 in the Nam Theung Village near the leg of Phou Bia. Two unidentified aircraft fired rockets that exploded on the ground, releasing a red and yellow substance that left holes in leaves and killed 28 people.

The U.S. government received a report of continuous bombardment over a 7-day period during the week of June 5, 1976 in the Pou Matao area. Two Ravens fired rockets that released a red and green substance, injuring 110 people and killing 40. Source was hit by both, lost an eye and has several keloids due to shrapnel injuries.

The U.S. government received a report of an attack on October 13, 1977 in the Phu Hay area south of Phou Bia. An L-19 aircraft fired 6 rockets releasing a yellow-gray substance that killed 25 people. Source visited the site after the attack and witnessed corpses with yellowish skin and yellowish discharge from their nose and mouth. Source's child who accompanied him drank water from the attack site and died about 2 hours later.

The U.S. government received a report of an attack on February 2, 1978 in the Tam Sé Sam Liem area of eastern Phou Bia. Two L-19 aircraft fired rockets and gas, releasing a yellow and black substance that injured 60 and killed 24 people.

The U.S. government received a report of an attack in February 1978 at 1200 hours in the Ban Nam Luk area south of Phou Bia. Two L-19 aircraft released a yellow and white substance that killed over 500 people. Those who drank contaminated water died within 3 hours, those who breathed the gas died within 12 hours.

The U.S. government received a report of an attack on February 16, 1978 at 1400 hours 20 kilometers southeast of Phou Bia by an L-19 aircraft that released a yellow substance killing 2 water buffaloes and 7 people. Four hours after the attack, source witnessed corpses that appeared to be asleep except for yellow discharge from the nose and mouth.

The U.S. government received a report of an attack on April 6, 1978 in the Tha Se area of Phou Bia. Two Raven O-1s fired 6 rounds that exploded in the air, releasing a yellow substance. Two of the source's children died.

Environmental problem until they are detoxified.

The U.S. government received a report of an attack on May 17, 1978 in the Phu Nam area. An L-19 Raven made 2 passes and dropped 2 bombs during each pass. The poison bombs were followed by an artillery attack that occurred in Muang Cha about four kilometers away from the bomb drop. Eighteen people were killed. There were no indications of blood nor fragment wounds on the dead bodies but swollen necks.

The U.S. government received a report of an attack on April 9, 1978 in the Ban Nangeun and Ban Simtian areas. Enemy troops launched an attack that included an L-19 aircraft with rockets, killing 100 people.

The U.S. government received a report of an attack on May 19, 1978 in the Pha Phai area. A light observation aircraft was observed overhead dropping an unknown substance. Villagers attempted to flee and relocate to an area about kilometers west. Not all people made it. In addition to others, source's oldest son, 19 years old and his daughter, 4 years were killed in the attack.

The U.S. government received reports of attacks between June – July 1978 in the Ban Don area. An aircraft with a jet engine released a yellow substance that killed 25 people. Corpses bled from the eyes and mouth.

The U.S. government received reports of attacks between June 21 – July 7, 1978 in the Phou Lan foothills of Phou Bia. A light observation aircraft with rockets flew 4 missions per day and released an unknown substance that injured 41 people and killed 76.

The U.S. government received a report of numerous attacks over a 4-month period starting on August 8, 1978 in the Nam Kai and Pha Koi areas. Supported by artillery operations on the ground, aircraft armed with 6 to 8 rockets flew about 15 missions daily, releasing about 300 rockets, both ordinary and gas types, killing 276 people.

The U.S. government received a report of an attack in early-September 1978 in the Nam Tia area. Two L-19 aircraft fired 4 rockets 4 times a day for 7 days, first shooting high explosive rockets and then gas rockets each time, releasing a yellow substance that injured 2 and killed 17 people.

United States has a large stockpile of lethal chemical munitions and agents to deter another country

Munitions and bulk containers filled with nerve agents and mustard gas

Stored in eight continental U.S. and two overseas locations

Found that improvements were needed in inspection and disposal of the stockpile maintenance...and disposal of the stockpile

...the stockpile is deteriorating

Condition of the stockpile is unknown

The U.S. government received a report of an attack on October 23, 1978 six kilometers north of Phou Khao west of Phou Bia. An L-19 aircraft fired 6 rockets, 5 of which exploded like fog shells. The sixth rocket burst above the treetop emitting a red gas. Because an airplane had overflown the village prior to the attack, villagers had dispersed so none were affected. But animals died with most showing [signs] of blood flow from the nose and mouth.

The U.S. government received a report of an attack on October 30, 1978 in the Phou Bia area. Two Raven 0-1s made a single pass and dropped 4 rockets, 2 of which exploded above the ground and 2 at tree-tops releasing a yellow green substance that killed 3 people. Victims vomited [...] had convulsions, then died.

The U.S. government received a report of an attack in October 1978 [...] north of Pho[u] [...] was 5 kilometers from the attack. Two [...] aircraft each fired 3 rockets that released yellow grey smoke. The attack occurred 5 days after [...] village leaders [...] enemy forces prepared to surrender to communist control.

The U.S. government received a report of an attack in [...] 1978 [...] Phou Bia [...] rockets released [...] with [...] injured 10 [...] people and killed [...] girl exposed burst with [...] with some drainage [...] liquid...Both her [...] died in the attack [...]

The U.S. government received a report of an attack on November 1978 in the Phou Xang Noi near Long Tieng. Two MiGs released a blue and yellow substance that killed 80 people. There was no military pressure on the village, however, 5 days after the gas attack, the village was hit by artillery.

[...] government received a report of an attack on November 1978 in the Phou Bia area. [...] is a US Foreign Service Officer who observed an unidentified plane drop a bomb that released a yellow substance...Source saw 2 victims who reached his position after the attack. The victims died about 2 hours later...Milk-like substance flowed from their mouth after death.

The U.S. government received a report of an attack in April 1979 in the Ban Nong Po area. [...] a yellow-brown [...] there was [...] in the Ban Don area [...] help...6-man [...] as [...] dying from fever...[if] the village were attacked again, that it had better shoot down the plane for proof.

Testing of a non-discernible microbioinoculator (device for clandestine inoculation with BW/CW agents)...cannot be identified structurally or easily detected upon a detailed autopsy

Special testing program for determining the lethality of the chemical filler

Army has demilitarized and disposed of large quantities of usable lethal chemical agents and munitions

Army has prepared a long-range plan for eventually disposing of the entire existing stockpile

Spent over $150 million to demilitarize and dispose...may spend $640 million to $870 million more

MKNAOMI

The U.S. government received a report of an attack on May 15, 1979 in the Ban Pha Ngam and Ban Pha Pou areas. Source is a Hmong resistance fighter who said that the Hmong fought back bravely against the enemy. An L-19 aircraft released a yellow, red, and white substance that killed 36 people. An unspecified number of people fled panic stricken into the jungle and dispersed.

The U.S. government received a report of an attack in April 1979 in the Ban Kosi area. Source went to buy rice five days after an attack and found many sick villagers. Over people had died

The U.S. government received a report of an attack on May 30, 1979 in the Muong Phong areas. A Raven aircraft fired two high rockets that released a red substance that injured and killed 3 people of the village five days after the attack and two villagers were torture and killed.

The U.S. government received a report of an attack in 1979 in the phou Phia area. An aircraft looked like an L-19 released a yellow substance killed 100 people. Source is a resistance fighter who plans to returns to Laos.

Says the United States may have made up the story about yellow rain to cover its own chemical arms use there

The U.S. government received a report of an attack between October 9-14, 1979 in the Ban Pha Koi area. An L-19 aircraft, accompanied by 130 MM artillery fire, bombarded a village with 122 MM rockets that released a white, red, green substance killing 32 people. The rest of the villagers fled the area and arrived to Thailand on October 20, 1979 by crossing the Mekong River.

Our understanding that all these materials were destroyed in compliance

We cannot, however, locate records that establish this fact

encouraged [Meo]to accept our assistance for our own purposes

Until 1967, the activities of the Meo were not particularly troublesome to North Vietnamese

If we had not involved ourselves in support of the Meo it is probable that they would largely have been left to their mountain ways

I am unable to bring myself to feel that the Meo would be necessarily much worse off had we left them alone

To varnish what is an essentially sad story

To varnish what is an essentially sad story

Told him that the Army had dumped in Southeast Asia many of its aging chemical weapons that were leaking in hopes of avoiding a panic about unsafe conditions back home

He saw American prisoners of war in Laos in 1981 — thinks U.S. officials murdered and lied to cover up the use of chemical and biological weapons in Southeast Asia after the Vietnam War

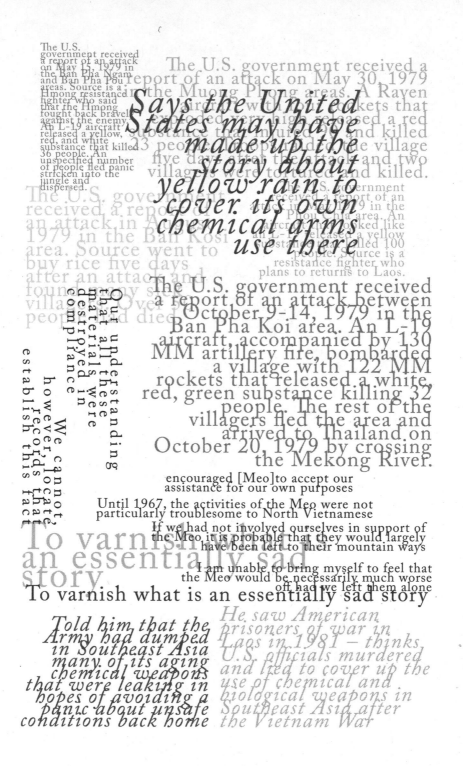

Late 1970s to mid-1980s. Hmong refugees provided blood, urine, vomit, sputum, breast milk, leaves, twigs, rock scrapings, clothing, and a two-month-old aborted fetus, all sent to laboratories for testing.

Then came shipping delays, specimens lost in transit, broken vials, backlogs of samples, and a lack of agency coordination. In this manmade confusion, the samples began to deteriorate. The government lacked the ability to fully test some of the specimens, so they rerouted samples to academic scientists.

July 1981. Dr. Chester Mirocha at the University of Minnesota found on a leaf sample strange levels of trichothecene mycotoxins, a fatal substance that can grow naturally in crops and plants, or develop from fungi and mold.

September 1981. Journalist Sterling Seagrave had written a book on yellow rain's connection to mycotoxins, slated for publication on September 24.

September 13, 1981. Less than two weeks before the book's release, Secretary of State Alexander Haig unexpectedly told the press while in Berlin: the US had evidence to prove the Soviet Union and its allies violated the Biological Weapons Convention (BWC) treaty by using biological weapons against refugees in Southeast Asia and Afghanistan. The treaty banned the storage, procurement, manufacture, and development of biological weapons or toxins, but failed to include compliance checks. The Geneva Protocol of 1925, a treaty forbidding the use of chemical and biological weapons, was also called into question.

December 1981. Dr. Joseph Rosen at Rutgers University tested and found the same substance as Mirocha, along with what might have been polyethylene glycol, a synthetic ingredient perhaps used to strengthen the toxin and its delivery.

1983 to 1986. The US sent to Southeast Asia a joint-agency team of State Department and Defense officials who found inconsistencies in the Hmong testimonies, stories told and then recanted. Their final report: not enough information to make a case for or against yellow rain. The United Nations also came back empty: it could not confirm or deny whether anything happened to the Hmong. As if to say to us: we don't really know if you died.

Blood Cooperation

> *. . . upset that they have learned nothing about the results of blood samples which they have provided. In their culture, Hmong traditionally hold that the body is unable to replace blood it has lost.*
>
> —**Cable from the US Embassy, Bangkok, to the Secretary of State, October 28, 1983**

> *. . . are not optimistic at this point that the Hmong community will cooperate on a large enough scale to satisfy our scientific requirements.*
>
> —**Cable from the US Embassy, Bangkok, to the Defense Intelligence Agency, April 19, 1984**

You've already scorned our hillsides,
Stripped into the ecology of our songs.

Now you beg for our blood, beseech us
Down to bruising kernel with no valley

To reclaim our roofs, no origin of iron
To bloom our vascular spool, as you draw

Out notions to be satiated at the supper
Waiting inside your scope, leave us in a

Daze to wander these camps in a state
Of vague withholding. This is our state

Of frozen knowing, the taking that
Happens in spite of all you've already

Spent. Blighted of our earliest silt, there
Is no more believing to give, not another

Cracked container to cast your claims.
We've no more tempers to shed for your

Pretense of goodwill, no more gloom
For the survival of your grander good.

Specimens from Ban Vinai Camp, 1983

1. Male, 18
Sample collected 11 Jan. 1983
Date of Exposure: Oct. 82

Blood (heparin) from brew of the fennel equinox x 1

Blood (clotted) from desire of a rusted persimmon x 1

Urine from force of an untouched nestling, a barefaced songbird x 2 (1 with acetone 1 salted within tone rupturing into alchemy)

2. Chemical Material Sample collected 12 Apr. 1982 at SG-98-33
Arrived BVC 6 Jan. 1983
Arrived Bangkok 12 Jan. 1983

(Small trines of stucco and rose quartz rising) hovering atop midheaven in a glass bottle

3. Chemical material collected 13 Oct. 1982, 1 km south of Pho Nou TF 74-78
Arrived BVC 7 Jan. 1983
Arrived Bangkok 12 Jan. 1983

(Carcassed blossoms mapped with yellow powder) in tin foil bag

4. Chemical material

Brought out of Laos 19 Jan. 1983 in a bamboo case by antennae of a moth

5. Male, 30
Sample collected 21 Jan. 1983
Last exposure in Laos to "chemical rain": Nov. 1982

Blood (heparin) from breath of a conifer of the most feral cold

Blood (clotted) from ecru river embodied once as an elder lake

Urine from template recollections transmuted into soul-print informatics

6) Male, 22
Sample collected 20 Jan. 1983
Last exposure in Laos to: Chemi? Nov. 1982

Blood (heparin) from wildness of clairancient pulp

Blood (clotted) from a flash of fire in pilgrimage to source

Urine from (urine and acetic acid) linguistics adrift and dissolved into ephemera

7) Female, 1 (daughter of ▆▆▆▆▆▆)
Last exposure to chemi in Laos: Nov. 1982

Urine from house of nephrite and coronated wheat

8) Female, 25
Sample collected 20 Jan. 1983
(Had an infant born 10 Jan. 1983)

Blood (heparin) from lunar flame spilling into seasons of lower winter

Blood (clotted) from threshold of higher arrival hidden in the crosswind

Lactating milk from drought of the heart's whistle

9) Female, 4 (daughter of ▆▆▆▆▆▆)
Sample collected 21 Jan. 1983

Blood (clotted) from aubade of every sunrise as membrane and memory, of each tempered stone fitted to its path, all luminance in apprentice to night's deep hues, every push of implied light, every thrust return

10) Female, 40
Sample collected 22 Jan. 1983
Last exposure to chemi in Laos: Nov. 1982

Blood (clotted) from auction of relinquished swear

Blood (heparin) from jasper seasonings of noctiflorous synchrony

Urine + acetic acid from sugar-throated evanescence

Lactating milk from blessings crested

11) Male, 4 (son of ▮▮▮▮▮▮▮▮▮▮ *)*
Sample collected 24 Jan. 1983

Blood (clotted) from forfeiting of climate

Blood (heparin) from glimmering peripheries inherited to those spited under their own sky

Questions:

At what temperature should blood, urine, and milk be kept while being stored and during transit?

Is lactating milk a suitable sample?

Have urine samples been rendered useless because of high acetic acid content?

How do we discern the nameless in order to veil what we know?

When was this deviance patented into truth?

What if we never forgive ourselves?

Why here and now?

These bones and children?

Can it be that a starving ripped the earth extensive to quench from it the last drops of milk?

Authorization to Depart Ravaged Homeland as Biomedical Sample

flew you afar   piecemealed

bits of spleen   liver   tissues of the second

gut orphaned   by the whole

routed you in a vacutainer ||

bangkok | frankfurt delayed | dulles | fort detrick

as if only born   to serve in

postmortem   detain offerings of

cerebral shards   to be juried under a lens

flew you | from the silken

wilderness | of | your | viscera

from all   the vacated

leftovers of yourself   sinews snipped |

culled   from the ribs | . in this   mission of guilt for

your unleaving   you've trekked

far from the village   salvaged in | sides   from you

and other hundreds   sealed on letter | head

dispersed to the globe | here at long   last in these united

states   you did not land a body

only | as a vial of blood | were you registered

as urine   did they label you   : asylum

sample M-35-82 | victim "7" en
route to london

fluids of you granted fare to

enter   refugee airspace

while ending away   in hospital camp

stayed behind   the | sourced | you

and every
else
part

sample M-25-82 | victim "9"
no weekend courier   ambiguously arriving

so stomach   of laments

||||| *how could they not*
get you here somehow

only   drops

relayed: lab   to: lab | to: lab

cargo of you | quaking   inside

an ice chest

Arriving as Lost

... it will be unaccompanied from Frankfurt to New York. ... Bangkok courier service indicates that no one has contacted ▇▇▇▇▇▇▇ *at State Dept in Washington* ▇▇▇▇▇▇▇ *Courier service indicates that it is imperative someone be in New York when Lufthansa Flight 404 arrives on 22 August at 1555 and that they have a ramp pass. Samples are being transported in the loose baggage hold where live animals travel. Courier service is concerned that unless this box is collected as soon after the aircraft lands as possible (prior to normal baggage off-loading procedures) it will go to the Port Authority and it will take a great deal of time to extricate it from this bureaucracy.*

—Cable from the US Defense Attaché Office, Bangkok, to the US Army Medical Intelligence and Information Agency, August 20, 1980

There's no defense for how they will
Fail you, how you will become

Trapped in movement among the
Turmoil of belongings. There's no

Reason for how no one will be there
To meet you, hold you onward,

Call you from the factory of your
Crossing. There's no acceptance for

Why you've been crammed alongside
Pets, placed haphazard to fend among

The crates. No belief for no one taking
You over continents, no explaining

Why you could result in a port, no
Mercy as to why no one has been told.

There will be zero persistence to
Confess into proof, not a sliver behind

To retrieve, but a box of broken vials
They never meant to find, taken as

The ransom for a mislaid answer
They never meant to receive.

Ever Tenuous

1980 July 24

(CLOTTED). THE FOLLOWING ADDITIONAL INFORMATION IS FURNISHED:
(1) TEST TUBES BROKEN AND CRACKED: ITEMS 3, 7, 8, 9, 10, 11, 15,
16, 17, 20 AND ONE UNNUMBERED.
(2) SAMPLES MISSING: ITEMS 12 AND 19.
(3) DUPLICATES: TWO SAMPLES IDENTIFIED AS NUMBER 5. (ONE TEST TUBE
HAS A VERY SMALL AMOUNT OF BLOOD AND IT APPEARS THAT A SECOND SAMPLE
WAS TAKEN FROM THE SAME PATIENT.)

DURING
TRANSIT, THE LARGE PIECES OF DRY ICE MOVED FREELY IN THE CONTAINER,
DAMAGING THE BLOOD SAMPLE TEST TUBES.

THE SAMPLES POSE A COMPLEX PROBLEM TO THE RESEARCH COMMUNITY
(CHEMICAL AND MEDICAL) BECAUSE THERE ARE NO TECHNIQUES, WITHIN THE
STATE-OF-THE-ART, TO POSITIVELY IDENTIFY A CHEMICAL AGENT THROUGH
AN ANALYSIS OF BLOOD, SPUTUM, URINE OR VOMIT.

1980 December 12

FOR YOUR INFORMATION, THE ABRIN SAMPLES FORWARDED TO FSTC WERE MISROUTED TO OUR AGENCY.   THE SAMPLES WERE HAND-CARRIED TO CSL ON 10 DEC 80.

1983 January 3

Contents spilled; container was rinsed with water and the water was analyzed for T-2 and HT-2 residue.

1983 February 1

2.   (C)   SAMPLE TH830121AC09 WAS SPILLED IN TRANSIT DUE TO IMPROPER PACKAGING AND IS NO LONGER OF ANY ANALYTIC VALUE.

1984 February 22

SUBJECT SAMPLES REPORTED BY REF A ABOVE DID NOT ARRIVE DULLES
INTERNATIONAL AIRPORT PER SCHEDULE PROVIDED. THIS OFFICE TRIED
TO NO AVAIL TO TRACE THE SHIPMENT. AMERICAN AND NORTHWEST
AIRLINES INDICATED THE ATP BILL NUMBER "012438044" IS NOT A
COMPLETE NUMBER (ONE DIGIT MISSING).

1984 May 9

Analysis is not planned on 72 specimens broken in
shipment and the 162 specimens for which we have no background.

1984 October 10

Results from two samples are missing, 1B-9 and 1B-14, from Table 2.
We are unable to locate these samples and an illness of one of our
staff members may have ~~been~~ caused   the loss. Also the T-2
tetraol result from IU-13 cannot be located.

1984 October 25

```
                    TH841004-121MS      BLOOD (CRACKED IN SHIPMENT)
                    TH841004-122MS      BLOOD (CRACKED IN SHIPMENT)
                    TH841004-123MS      URINE
                    TH841004-124MS      BLOOD
                    TH841004-125MS      BLOOD (CRACKED IN SHIPMENT)
               TH841004-126MS           URINE
                    TH841004-127MS      BLOOD (CRACKED IN SHIPMENT)
                    TH841004-128MS      BLOOD (CRACKED IN SHIPMENT)
                    TH841004-129MS      URINE
                    TH841004-130MS      BLOOD (CRACKED IN SHIPMENT)
                    TH841004-131MS      BLOOD
                    TH841004-132MS      URINE
                    TH841004-133MS      BLOOD
                    TH841004-134MS      BLOOD
                    TH841004-135MS      URINE (2 PARTS)
```

1984 October 31

ARRIVED IN A DEPLORABLE CONDITION. ALL SAMPLES HAD THAWED. THIRTY PERCENT OF THE GLASS TUBES CONTAINING BLOOD WERE BROKEN AND LEAKING. THIS RESULTED IN A SERIOUS BIOLOGICAL HAZARD WHICH COULD HAVE BEEN AVOIDED IF THE RECOMMENDED PROCEDURES HAD BEEN FOLLOWED. AFMIC WILL NOT ACCEPT FUTURE BLOOD SAMPLE SHIPMENTS UNLESS THEY ARE PROPERLY PACKAGED.

IF POSSIBLE, BACKGROUND IS NEEDED FOR SAMPLE NUMBERS TH-841121-1MS THROUGH TH-841121-5MS. WERE THESE VICTIMS OR CONTROLS AND WERE PHYSICAL EXAMS DONE? UPON ARRIVAL OF THE FOUR ICE CHESTS AT AFMIC THERE WAS NO DRY ICE LEFT. SAMPLES IN SIX OF THE CANS UNPACKED WERE STILL FROZEN, SAMPLES IN ONE WERE PARTIALLY FROZEN, AND SAMPLES IN ONE WERE COMPLETELY THAWED BUT STILL COLD.

2. (C) REF {B}, IF NO BACKGROUND IS AVAILABLE FOR SAMPLE NUMBERS TH-841124-1MS THROUGH TH-841124-14MS NO ANALYSIS WILL BE DONE. YOU MAY DESTROY THESE SAMPLES.

. . . must see the victims sooner. Typically it takes a Hmong 4-6 weeks to travel from his village to Thailand.

—**Trip Report to the US Army Biomedical Laboratory, October 23, 1979**

. . . after a few days at room temperature growth of bacteria is likely to spoil the usefulness of the samples.

—**Cable from the Foreign Science and Technology Center to the US Defense Attaché Office, Bangkok, July 10, 1980**

. . . we are becoming far from convinced that even if we happen upon a Hmong who reports exposure within two weeks, that we can, through clinical evidence, determine that he was or was not exposed to CW.

—**Cable from the US Defense Attaché Office, Bangkok, to the Defense Intelligence Agency, January 29, 1981**

The possibility that the toxic substance(s) were present initially but unstable in storage cannot be completely ruled out.

—**Cover letter to the Army Medical Research and Development Command, June 4, 1982**

. . . there can be no doubt that 10027-G originally contained high levels of both T-2 and DAS. The failure of two relatively inexperienced laboratories to detect those toxins after the sample has aged for two years is not surprising.

—**Cable from the Armed Forces Medical Intelligence Center to the Foreign Science and Technology Center, March 14, 1983**

Only those individuals sampled within one to three months after the alleged attack still showed mycotoxins. . . . There are 64 different trichothecenes known and it is impossible at present to test for all of these.

—**Cable from the Armed Forces Medical Intelligence Center, April 23, 1984**

They colluded you to behave
     As if you had not happened

Thawed your wasteland from their
     Trafficked conscience

To groom a marionette of thumbs
     The answer is to ask

Who concocted you not sprung
    From a lineage of honeybees

Swimming into the sterile
    Negation of your breath

Tricksters who forged you from
    The gut of their contriving

Smugging open the cells of their
    Schemed imaginings

They make you indefinite
    Make you drive them

Pointless until no hint of potion
    Remains as proof

But a game of science jigsawed
    To certify your absence

And choke their own distrust
    That even in their doubt

Despite the weeks months
    You'd been there all along

This gamble of a deadline wrought
    From a sickened eloquence

You were concrete strung
    Your mouth alive

While they swayed you
    Dense as topsoil into fern

Procedures in Hunt of Wreckage

I.

Summary of Results: Positive for T-2 toxin
Source: Blood
Analysis Performed: T-2 Toxin, HT-2 Toxin, DAS
Results and Conclusions:

First precipitated with acetone and then filtered

> We have no clue what we
> are involved in. The hum
>
> that sieves and slithers amid
> our wildfire lips has already
>
> dampened to the sea.

Filtrate evaporated to dryness, dissolved in
methanol-water, passed through an XAD-2 column

> We're in a thread to misinform,
>
> on track to baffling the facts,
> assuming what we know
> of the sky.

90% methanol eluate collected, dried on a steambath

> Leading out from the stream
>
>   plaited and lit
> by a scorpion in the stars.

Gas chromatograph-mass spectrometer data system

> How much lies before us
> we quantify as antiquity.

To split time at its limbs,
a cadre of quills, woodlands

uncoiled,
>   house of twine
>   screaming ill for its queen.

II.
Source: Vegetative samples
Analyses Performed: T-2 toxin, H-2, DAS
Results and Conclusions:

Leaf samples were extracted with ethyl acetate

>   How much in our doing
>   to taste futility.

Concentrated redissolved in acetonitrile

>   Not tell anyone
>   how extraordinary this
>   brink, how devastated
>   we are, how needled
>   we break.

Partitioned with petroleum ether

>   What sorcery of microbiology
>   proves the tolerance of sorrow.

>   How will our process confirm
>   the existence of death. Measures

>   to misuse the period of torrents.
>   What methods to mitigate

>   the suffering of a mountain
>   that has deserted its own wrist.

To dryness then dissolved, concentrated to 20 ml

> War-doing is a cycle
> of trial and error.
>
> Death-giving is permission
> to trial and error.

Loaded onto an XAD column and eluted with 90% methanol

> Loaded single file
> into a vault of earth and calcite, women
> and children farthest to the back.

Collected and dried for analysis by GC-MS

> Collected to launder one
> nation under God from
> disease of ourselves.
>
> Collected and condoled
> for storage in the month
> of scarcity and fallen feasts.

Disfigures

The delay in funding . . . is having a serious negative effect on the team's substantive work. Over the past five months, the team has been functioning by bleeding other mission elements for transportation, vehicles, and secretarial support. . . . At present, we do not even have the funds or fiscal authority to purchase the sodium fluoride required to preserve human blood samples, thus hampering the team's efforts at a time when we should be most alert to collection possibilities.

—**Cable from the US Embassy, Bangkok, to the Secretary of State, March 2, 1984**

Unless immediate action is taken to provide these resources, sample analysis will come to a halt due to lack of funds.

—**Memo by the Armed Forces Medical Intelligence Center, May 9, 1984**

It's about the money	It's not about the money
It's about politics	It's not about the politics
It's about budget restraints	It's not about budget restraints
It's about proving yellow rain	It's about disproving yellow rain
It's about men and their need for more arms	It's about men and their need to repurpose arms
It's about men and their need for power	It's about controlling access to power
It's about concocting the reason to shore up	It's about dismantling the reason to shore up
It's about leveraging the Hmong story of yellow rain	It's about rejecting the Hmong story of yellow rain as lies
It's about routing blood samples in a timely manner	It's about misrouting, delays, loss of sample integrity
It's about taking down the Soviets	It's about defending the Soviets
It's about violating treaties	It's about ignoring violations
It's about how to grade compliance of treaties	It's about the façade of compliance

More than prototyping
Means of sabotage

Experimentation of new
Concealments

It's about the footprint of bees
Collectors of a pearled stock

Unable to send
Their wings into bloom

It's about a face
No longer to wake a disheveled

Neck staring through the satin
Of its own shadow

It's about a shroud of guilt
Theaters of espionage to

Sour and scandalize
Cider of the sun

It's about the money
The currency of a body

The body as a form
Of currency

It's about buildup

A collection of stiff bodies
In a cemetery of debt

Request for Furthermore

We are nowhere near deduction.

Further from conclusion coming up void.

Please collect new blood and urine samples.

Taut with higher harm to be ionized into staggered lies.

> *Match age, sex, general state of*
> *health, and . . . diet history of each*
> *individual with that of a control*

Give us anything you can.

> *Collect samples of any traditional*
> *or herbal medicines*

Give us *dietary samples.*

Clan labels.

The accent they share with roosters.

Give us the placentas they give to their gods.

> *We really need control samples*
> *from the refugee population*

Objects fermented.

Peppers of the sunset meal.

Granules of catalyst mold.

Clothing samples are urgently needed

Try to match to best of your ability
the degree of wear of the item

Ragged textures bolting unkempt.

The man wearing two shirts.

As well, give us the shirt underneath.

Archive of rare clouds.

We need a collage. Credible ephemera.

At your discretion: a loop of hair, tendon of embedded aloe, wept hugs inside a thimble.

Please send medical records, results of any
diagnostic tests, blood workups, physician
notes; in short, anything that will provide
additional details on the individual's
physical condition

Any of these conditions:
> Unsterile ennui
> A cloned delusion of relief
> Pain of the instinct to flee
> Hollowness
> Plight of wounded movement

We are particularly interested in whether
or not skin lesions have developed

Please consider we are asking for conundrums.

Consider our backlog a scrapbook of scattered strangers.

We are overwhelmed.

Falling through in vain from the fever of this work.

In need of more giving.

Whatever to uphold we've unlocked the lion's coffer.

Whatever to gorge from the kill in its gut.

We Can't Confirm Yellow Rain Happened, We Can't Confirm It Didn't

And just as it cannot be stated here that the allegations are confirmed, neither can it be stated that on the evidence available, they can be rejected.

—**Paper by J. P. Perry Robinson, March 1980**

. . . quite possible for the investigation to fail to achieve its objective.

—**Memo from the Department of the Army, Office of the Surgeon General, to the Under Secretary of Defense for Research and Engineering, August 29, 1980**

. . . neither confirmation nor denial as to exposure to a chemical warfare agent can be made. —**Report from the US Army Medical Intelligence and Information Agency, November 18, 1980**

Whereas the group could not state that these allegations had been proven, nevertheless, it could not disregard the circumstantial evidence suggestive of the possible use of some sort of toxic chemical substance.

—**Cable from the US Mission of the United Nations, Chemical Weapons Experts Team, New York, to the Secretary of State, December 1, 1982**

Conclusive *proof of Soviet supply of the chemical agents is still lacking. . . . [S]uch proof is unlikely to be acquired.*

—**CIA Special National Intelligence Estimate Report, March 2, 1983**

An honest two-word assessment of the data that we have on hand for FY 83 and 84, in my opinion, is "inconclusive junk."

—**Memo by Sharon A. Watson, toxicologist and lead yellow rain investigator at AFMIC, July 5, 1985**

. . . but these results neither confirm nor deny the use of mycotoxins as CW agents. . . . In some instances, as long as three weeks had passed between the attack and the collection of samples, and three to four more weeks had elapsed during return of samples to Canada. During that time, no precautions were taken to preserve the samples.

—**Cable from the US Embassy, Bangkok, to the Secretary of State, April 3, 1986, regarding Canada's report on results**

Unless [the data] are assessed in the context of all the relevant data . . . they are, at best, inconclusive and, at worst, misleading.

—**Memo from the Armed Forces Medical Intelligence Center to the CBW Use Committee, May 14, 1986**

We've reached   an impasse.

Flawed   psithurism in the night fall

                chanting rumors   we will fail

crash ourselves   beyond the caution   of saintly balm.

        Expert-bounding   between what we know

                and what they've told   we can sell

    you this much fact: these people   forever canceled out

        in a perpetual   chasm of   in-between

immortal   vacillation

                of now and never   never there nor here

        dead nor alive   accepted nor rejected

fled nor home.

        We don't have the means   to give up the absolute.

Too much   drains at stake   to ratify our own   absurdity.

        Announce our verdict   of confusion   we cannot

        plan   the uninvited   but to blend

dichotomies of truth   brain-drowsed   junked out

                crude   to concede.

        We   an   impressive   debacle.

                Here lie
                the ashes

                of our
                        sanity.

Composition 2

people seemed "drunk" and died in a few hours
"shake" all over (like chills)
breathing painful—more so with inhaling
dizzy with desire to vomit
secondary infection in skin lesions
many "bruises" on skin—questionable hemorrhages
eyes, tearing and reddening and blurred vision

throat felt hot and dry
stomach was upset, he vomited and had diarrhea
small blisters which changed from red to black
fell over
vomited and had diarrhea with blood
gas blisters appeared
pepper-like feeling in the nose and throat
entire body became swollen
burning in nose followed by bleeding
blood yellow sputum
diarrhea (4-5 times per day for 12 days)
vomiting (5-6 times per day for 10 days)

vomiting   hemorrhage
diarrhea   breathing difficulty
itching and skin irritation   paralysis
dry mouth   dizziness
tremors or convulsions
rapid loss of consciousness
rash or blisters   tearing
facial edema   coughing
tachycardia   nausea   sweating
headache   blurred vision   fatigue
hearing loss   skin color change
nasal excretion   loss of appetite   salivation
temporary blindness

*indications that the use
of these lethal agents is
e x p e r i m e n t a l*
*soldiers wearing protective
masks entered a strike area
immediately after an attack*

*several chemicals being used
are mixed together in a
variety of concentrations*

*dispersed in various
patterns*

*injected survivors with a
solution apparently being
tested as an antidote*

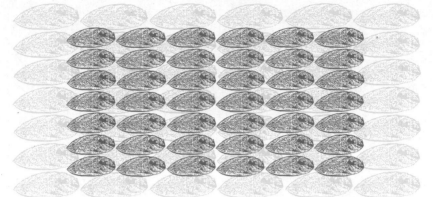

1. nausea vomiting severe immediate   nausea vomiting severe immediate .1
2. "falling down" world turning   dizziness .2
3. small blisters burning of skin erythema with burning sensation of skin .3
4. shaking all over   ataxia occasional tremors convulsions .4
5. bleeding eyes   congestion of sclera and blood in tears .5
6. pounding chest   hypotension with rise in heart rate .6
7. pain in chest   angina .7
8. sleepiness   somnolence cns symptoms .8
9. bleeding gums inflammation of oral mucous membranes excessive salvation .9
10. difficulty breathing   shortness of breath .10
11. skin hot with cold   fever and chills .11
12. diarrhea with blood   diarrhea with blood .12
13. bleeding into skin and fingernails   thrombocytopenia and purpura .13
14. drop in white blood cell count   leukopenia and anemia .14
15. rotten stomach intestines   rapid necrosis of linings of GI tract .15
16. swelling of organs   congestion of all organs .16

...useful to begin an epidemiological study of the effect of CBW on births with a focus on spontaneous abortions, term birth deformities and infant death.

There are a large number of Hmong available at Ban Vi Nai to provide the raw data appropriate for such a study.

principal CIA program | research and development of chemical and biological agents | "concerned with the research and development of chemical, biological, and radiological materials capable of employment in clandestine operations to control human behavior"

MKULTRA

considered to be professionally unethical

fatigue, lack of appetite,
joint pain, death

weeks

skin lesions,
continuing diarrhea,
trembling, fatigue,
bruising, death

days

vomiting (with increasing amounts
of blood), diarrhea (with blood),
trembling, bleeding gums, edema,
skin rashes and blisters, death

hours

itching or
tingling of
the skin, eye
irritation

vomiting, dizziness, rapid
heartbeat, chest pain, vision
problems, feeling of intense
heat or burning of the skin

immediate

10 to 30 minutes

[Soviet] Operational testing
The local situations offer favorable
opportunities to evaluate the
effectiveness of weapons under
field conditions.

[Soviet] Operational testing
The local situations offer favorable
opportunities to evaluate the
effectiveness of weapons under
field conditions.

1 April 1974 | Dr. Richard Hammerschlag | a paper called
"Ethnic Weapons" | evidence to suggest that Pentagon
agencies | exploiting genetically-related susceptibilities and
intolerances in order to use germ or chemical weapons
selectively against certain populations

his discovery that screening of blood
proteins in various Asian populations
had recently received support from the
Advanced Research Projects (ARPA)
Project Agile…"an elite group of
civilian scientists conducting
high risk research…"

certain populations
certain populations
certain populations
certain populations
certain populations
high risk research
high risk research

"If we proceed without open air testing, we
find ourselves in the unenviable position of owning a
stockpile of chemical munitions whose efficiency has
never been demonstrated."

note that the vomiting described by the
refugees was often bloody, and at times
projectile with bright red blood
of the reported symptoms, 96% are consistent with T2

SECRET

MEMORANDUM FOR THE RECORD   14 June 1983

SUBJECT: Human Subjects Review Panel Procedures

On 24 May 1983 _____ DGC Advisor to the Panel, and I met
with _____ the Executive Director for purposes of discussing
Panel activities with him, and soliciting his views on procedures
for forwarding the Panel recommendations to the Director of Central
Intelligence. We discussed the history of the yellow rain project,
using that activity as an example.

Human Subjects
example   yellow rain
                          activity

project project project project project project
project project project project project project
project project project project project project

MEMORANDUM FOR: Chairman, Human Subjects Review Panel

FROM: Chairman, DCI/NIC CBW-Toxin Working Group

SUBJECT: Medical Screening Project ___

REFERENCE: Memorandum from _____
                 dated 25 April 1983   The Medical
                                              Policy Analysis is
        Director of the Institute for Foreign Policy Analysis is
                        , M.D. Harvard Medical School, a specialist in
        tropical medicine with board certification in Internal
        Medicine. In addition to language capability in Thai,
        some Hmong, and Khmer he has had extensive appropriate
        in-country experience.

                                              Science and Technology Division/OSWR

SUBJECT: Protection of Human Subjects of Chemical/Toxin
                 Weapons Screening Project

   1. This memorandum constitutes a progress report on the
above-mentioned project. At the present time, it appears that
the appropriate safeguards have been observed with respect to
the protection of human subjects.

   3. In March 1982, the Director of Central Intelligence
requested _____, STD/OSWR, to prepare a letter to
Dr. Teller concerning the proposal for special relief to victims
of chemical warfare in Thailand refugee war camps (Attachment A).
The Executive Director was involved in this matter in August 1982
(Attachment B). The original proposal involved experimentation and
treatment in addition to collection methods. The experimentation
and treatment aspects have since been removed. The collection of
human data however, appears to constitute research under the HHS
guidelines.   Health and Human Services (HHS)

whether examined in the
United States or abroad.

78

It was the Cold War, an era that gave way to political charades. The US versus the Soviet Union in a competition of two-faced antagonizing. To build a stockpile of mass destruction. To overthrow the earth.

1969. President Richard Nixon halted production of chemical biological weapons in a move to disarm the US.

Late 1970s to the 1980s. The administrations of Presidents Carter and Reagan moved toward rearming once again.

1987. The US resumes production of chemical weapons.

Dear Nixon, how do you properly disable a weaponized world?

Dear Carter, whose ancestral lands have suffered under the storage and keeping of this arsenal?

Dear Reagan, in whose lands will you pour and dispose of these poisons?

Dear Leader, where do we bury our—

Subterfuge

Maybe you spiked the dirt
With your snare of shivers.

You watched lemongrass
Retreat into the parasols,

Discarded this jungle into
The cinema of forgetting.

 You've been lying again.

Maybe you knew the venom
Had been painted, that it

Slipped beneath torn
Umbrellas, smothering all

Touch as a vapor buffet.
Honestly. A curse as this

Is a tribunal for the late
Uncles, the bemoaned first

Sons. How you must have
Felt embassy-like, diminishing

A species of servicemen for
An administration of wasps.

This Demands the Vengeance of a Wolf

The high level of metals detected by neutron activation analysis, particularly in the leaf sample, are indicative of special steels such as stainless steel, magnetic steel or other special purpose steels. This suggests that these samples were either processed and/or stored in steel containers. Iron, manganese, and chromium were detected. . . . [A] measurable quantity of cobalt, the major component in jet engine bearings, should be noted. This finding lends some support to the purported jet engine dissemination of aerosols.

— **Report of test results from the US Army Armament Research and Development Command, Chemical Systems Laboratory, March 25, 1981**

This suggests the fertile rage of planes

This suggests tufts of infectivity slumbering in a bomb

This suggests aiming from the domes of trees, periling without expense

This infers a means to sunder, a body made of daggers to defeat the uptight vantage

Here signifies the performance of a missive, dispensing kills of convenience to suckle an audience into erasure

This finding vaccinates with rings and waves of malachite

Splatted across the pillaged night sky, its tempo dismissed before it could learn to sing

This surmises a culprit

PROBABLE ENEMY METHODS OF DELIVERING BIOLOGICAL AGENTS

AIRCRAFT SPRAY

BOMBLETS FROM MISSILES

VECTORS

This enforces the complicity of headship

This suggests a book of haze as thick as
swimming into bits

What we can discern
and strip apart from
a leaf, how many sagas
of air, how deep the hours
under smolder, how disjointed
landings drink the tank of
its own torment, then be
found and given a faith,
ferocity in the cobalt
lifting toward redress

Agent Orange Commando Lava

One that leads to: another leads to: another: leads to: war crime

Pulling up furtive roots
A deep and definite frequency carved for

Children to dig and ignite their earnest way through

*

13 January 1967
Memorandum from the Deputy Under Secretary of State for Political Affairs Kohler to
Secretary of State Rusk

>   *Department of Defense phase of Operation Popeye*
>   *North Vietnam and southern Laos produce sufficient*
>   *rainfall along these lines of communication to interdict*
>   *or at least interfere with truck traffic*
>
>   *cloud seeding techniques non-publicized effort to*
>   *induce continued rainfall through the months*
>   *of the normal dry season*

Even the rain they think they own
Even the rain as casualty collateral
Price of their self-worth

Rain as refugee

>   *test phase of Project Popeye*
>   *conducted without consultation with Lao authorities*
>   *more than fifty cloud seeding experiments*
>   *outstandingly successful*

Mother Nature to labor
On their behalf

A climate in constant demise
In anxiety of karma to be dealt

>   would drastically change the weather patterns
>   life cycle of plants and animals may be affected
>   formation of fungi and growth of bacteria
>   could produce serious localized flooding

If this happened then why
Not yellow rain
            If these experiments then
    Why not yellow rain   If climatic
Repercussions resulting
                    From experiments
                            Then why
                            Not yellow rain

*

29 May 1967
Telegram from the Embassy in Laos to the Department of State

>   experiment in soil destabilization for the
>   purpose of producing impassable mud on
>   enemy lines of communication
>   has proved successful

How they'll defeat the enemy:
First prove they can defeat

The earth dismantled to add
An armed advantage against

            The home of the other

>   air-dropping common chemicals on two
>   interdiction points along Route 96 and Route 110

rain falling on these chemicals results in chelation
and dispersion of soil in such measure that mud

loses all consistency and becomes incapable of
supporting vehicles or any other substantial weight

They don't realize the sky
Never left the sky

Foothill still rises in the east

They can wash the blood from
Their sheets

      I would like to make mud on several routes in Laos

They cannot wash the dead
From their mind

      Who will forfeit themselves to the earth
Who of their own will pay the soil's tax

*

1 June 1967
Subject: Soil Destabilization Project

Now they've gone
And upset the dirt

      technical aspects of our COMMANDO LAVA project

      we have learned that Proctor and Gamble is test
      marketing a new detergent product called "Gain"

      without recognizing it, the Food and Drug
      Administration has given its blessing to our
      COMMANDO LAVA mix

That laundry should have
Everything to do with war and soil

What is there to benefit
But an imitation of clean

*

9 July 1982
Subject: Vietnamese report on US chemical warfare
charges that the US sprayed toxic chemicals including
Agent Orange and toxic gases included CS in Vietnam
in violation of the Geneva Protocol

It is not hard for them to always
Be in violation of something

caused ocular lesions, prolonged asthenia, congenital
anomalies and chromosomic alterations among the
inhabitants as well as killing 3,500 Vietnamese outright

There is no way they didn't know of these effects

They knew but did it anyway

*

If biology to be used against itself
            Then obviously yellow rain
                    If mutilating
            Science to
                    Militarize Mother Nature

legal, and perhaps moral or philosophical,
aspects to the question whether the US
should utilize the capability

If dearth of scruples

strictest secrecy
vulnerability to communist charges of
US manipulation of weather

The dead do tell
Then yellow rain then yellow rain

Toxicology Conference Proposal

Title of Panel:

        Martyr Your Lungs: Pulmonary Toxicology of the Mycotoxin

Presenter:

        Pathophysiology Division of the United States Army Medical Research Institute of Infectious Diseases, Fort Detrick, Maryland

Type of Study: *Inhalation*
Type of Toxicant: *Natural Products*
Type of Target: *Pulmonary*

Abstract: *. . . there are few documented toxicity data following respiratory exposure of T-2 toxin.*

But out here on the verge
where we fantasize with

our guiltless hands, feign
ignorance to carry on as

though we suffer from a
deficit, we've already built

what we need to know.
We've scored our studies.

We've aced our trials.
We've milked the tests

down to the barest bead
of soot.

The methodology for generating aerosols of T-2 mycotoxin . . . was developed.

      For distension of the airways,
      taken in by sprays, before

we waged ourselves to charade
the arena of our work, serving

death as an ode to scholarship,
we wrote this doctrine of rain

long before we knew the
afterwar would need it.

Rats and mice were exposed to T-2 mycotoxin both by inhalation and by intratracheal instillation . . .

So were refugees
exposed, treated

with specimen and
ambient outflow

underneath the
tripwire of our planes.

Time to death following respiratory exposure of T-2 mycotoxin . . . may vary from <0.5 hrs to >168 hrs.

Length of existence required
for disposal of the scene, razing

the mosaic to remove any
vestige of our having been there.

They won't find the print of our
heels. They won't even
smell our DNA.

Run the work, clean it up,

as if we inveigled ourselves
into prodigy, veneering the stain
on our palms.

Smear of Petals

Most inherited of all harbored
Plants, most coveted for your

Seeded healing, how have you
Become a charm of their constant

Scraping when you had only ever
Been a cure for ours? No longer

To hear moisture in the solstice,
They descended you elsewhere

Minus your numinous boughs,
Pulled from the shade of our

Hands. Tyrants they are to
Harvest your divinity then tonic

You as their swan. How eager they
Were to drink you. Soon enough,

It will happen. They will lose these
Battles and go home. They will let

Fall a blanket of choke on your
Fields, from their planes come

Down a riot of jaws, defoliant
Of their guilt, herbicide on you to

Cloak their crimes. Then you become
Yellow as the rain, disbursed,

A foreign hunger, padded in your
Power as sin of their design to

Sweep children in the way.

Syndrome Sleep Death Sudden

a.

*. . . over fifty previously healthy young adult Hmong males,
who emigrated and were living in the US, have died suddenly
in their sleep. Post-mortem examination of these cases have
demonstrated no cause of death. . . . [A]ll possibilities must be
considered . . .*

Perhaps you left it all   behind   your spirit
   in mid-flee   crawling   chaotic among
the perished.   Perhaps it was the

      calamity of mountains   maybe dream
  becoming memory   becoming electricity
serrated   out of your sleep.   No cause of why   you

   are no longer here   insults your   dying.
You lie   unheeded in your   gifting   after they've
    drawn the   sugar   from your veins.

b.

*Sleep disturbances. . . . [A]bnormal respirations . . . as gasp-
ing and groaning sounds, distinct from normal snoring. . . .
[O]ccurs in Asian populations that are culturally and geneti-
cally distinct. . . . Migrants from affected Asian populations
appear to carry with them the susceptibility to sudden death
in sleep.*

   Sound of your last   sound murmur of your
  last murmur   last   of your   last primordial grasping
   maybe we are   the ill ones   without skill

    to close our   eyes   misled in our   purpose
for lying down.   How much of what we are prone to
   does it take   to build   an ethnic   weapon?

c.

. . . autopsy results, of 39 (38 young men, 1 woman) US
sudden death victims (refugees from Southeast Asia) at the
Center for Disease Control in Atlanta last week. . . . Charges
have been made in the past that the deaths are delayed effects
associated with "yellow rain."

They will say   all points   lead to inconclusive
      no   definitive result on this   nor the toxins
  as though   after everything has been   stolen

      they will also   steal   the knowledge   of your death
and say   some bodies are bent   for dozing off
        in sleep.   They will say   they cannot discern

    contours of water   from   contours of a gulf
unable to slip their   fingers   through the difference
        to heed   that all dying   does not end up   the same.

Skin as a Vehicle for Experimentation

I.
Maze through connected whistles as a vehicle for incapacitating agents.

Vibration of thermal highness as a vehicle for incapacitating agents.

Diving into gothic flight as a vehicle for incapacitating agents.

Feathers in a vortex as a vehicle for incapacitating agents.

Blemish of flies as a vehicle for incapacitating agents.

Apis as a vehicle for incapacitating agents.

II.
It starts with skin, the vellum
to our fleshhood keeping us at
indivisible ease.

To dismantle the dermal fact,
they want to rip it down, anchor
apart the sleeve we fell into.

   ██████████ *is a chemical with
  the rather extraordinary property
  of penetrating skin rapidly*

Love on a stone path leading
to a pergola pouring down
wisteria *as a possible means of*

*delivering an incapacitating
chemical agent via the skin.*
This skin they cannot tear.

*The stratum corneum constitutes by far
the major part of the skin barrier . . .*

*If it can be breached, drugs can gain
entrance to the body via the skin . . .*

If it can be hacked, if they pilot
our bodies in search of ways
to sever our being, let everywhere

      come the muscles out of hiding.

III.
As a vehicle for asphyxia
of apology, as accuracy

given in its discounted
edition, as though dumped

and scalded in the acid
of their iniquities, there is

no evaporation as a vehicle
for incapacitating agents.

IV.
      *. . . the genital area would be an ideal target,
      since the scrotal and genital skin is likely to
      be more "permeable" to ▓▓▓▓▓▓▓ than
      skin in most other areas of the body. Various
      psychological factors would enter in here also.*

Take away   every epicenter   for a   target
    Take the body from the being   remove the casing

  from the throat   split the scars from its mortal
     cache   You have always   been beautiful

long before   they tested you as   permeable
and long after they   unfurled you from your vine

                   They'll take   what skin they   can
but not the skin of   your intuition

     Never the snowy shadow   of your highest might
This roughened web   cutaneous   cloth of human

              no longer to pine inside the   shallows

A Moment Still Waiting for You

Repeated description by medically unsophisticated victims
Properties that were ideal for chemical agents
Cannot reasonably and scientifically be attributed to a natural contamination
Firm conclusion that trichothecene mycotoxins are a component
Total composition of [yellow rain] is still unknown
Could not be the results of any natural phenomenon
Must have been the result of action by man

Come for all that belongs to you, all that waits for your unfeathered knowing in the anteroom of this information, a space becoming souvenir of the body's last bath to helix you into urgency as the remembering one. Open to receive everything you won't know so that in your uncertainty you will come across love. As when before you were born, it was sky times, we seemed to know our way around this labyrinth of air, drinking up seasons of the land with every new almanac of our lineage. We walked sensing our seamless cord to the roots above. It was always hard times but at least we were free, at least we could dream of you being free to live out the structures of your heart. But we are such a demographic of spirits in that our hearts have always been broken down through the path, such that now we are a scattering of evidence, siloed from the gravity that once held our knees firm to each other, such that we feed on the crumbs of our survival every time we go missing in beggary. When the great motion happened, before you came to partake in this earth's timing, many of us got caught in the rain and could not find our way scraping the storm with our skin. It was our flux to own, unable to meet the center but endlessly falling toward aphelion. This time of deep secrets we learned to put our trust in guessing, a waterfall born of mugwort, a meteor born of an ox, a rage born of a blade, a lesson born of cremation. It won't be long until you are born of the rug under the river, kicking open the book of your foe's timeline. You are not simply here, not simply present. What you are is not what anywhere expects of you. It's as subtle as an owl in astral flight that what you are is not here, not this, not ever, but only now.

For the Nefarious

From a recessed hollow
Rumble, I unearth as a creature

Conceived to be relentless.
Depend on me to hunt you

Until you find yourself
Counting all the uncorked

Nightmares you digested.
I will let you know the burning

Endorsed by the effort of
Matches. And you will claw

Yourself inward, toward a
Conference of heat as the steam

Within you surrenders, caves
You into a cardboard scar.

Even what will wreck you
Are your mother's chapped lips.

Even to drip your confession
Of empty rooms. I know about

Your recipe of rain, your apiary
Ways. Trust me to be painful.

Composition 3

Asian honeybee behavior had not been closely studied

did not know whether these bees defecated collectively

which is why it was the perfect weapon

Thailand in March 1984 | discovered that
wild honeybees | do indeed conduct
collective cleansing flights

spots later were shown to consist almost entirely of pollen

which is why it was the perfect weapon

levels of trichothecenes were found in the blood of five persons who
had not claimed exposure

April 1987 | Porton [Down] reported the natural occurrence of
trichothecenes | food crops from Thailand

which is why it was the perfect weapon

none of the alleged attacks was witnessed by a western observer

interviews with Hmong refugees from Laos
indicate the Hmong do not generally
recognize honeybee feces for what they are

which is why it was the perfect weapon

Nowicke had found | several plant families | common in Southeast Asia | no
two spots | had the same mixture of pollen types | not to be expected for a
chemical

Dr. Akratanakul | never
noticed bee feces deposits
in all his years of work
until the present yellow
rain controversy arose

indistinguishable from
the feces of wild Asian
honeybees

which is why it was the perfect weapon

it was the perfect weapon, which is why

little room to doubt | Hmong had frequently
mistaken | was, in fact, the feces

number of controls, the
manner and sequence in
which they were analyzed |
not adequately reported
which is why it
was the perfect weapon

not even in samples that the
Minnesota laboratory had
reported positive

which is why it
was the perfect
w e a p o n

government laboratories in the United States
(CSL) and the UK (Porton Down) were failing to
confirm which is why it was the perfect weapon

AFMIC argued that the trichothecenes
had decomposed

which is why

but pure T-2 and DAS are stable

it was the

no experimental evidence showing that they would
decompose in environmental samples under the
conditions

perfect weapon

problem of trichothecene instability does arise
it was the perfect weapon

does so in a manner that raises additional doubts about the
reliability of reports of trichothecenes in blood and urine
samples   it was the perfect weapon

was so rapid...useful only within the first 6 hr [six hours] following
exposure
which is why it was the
perfect weapon

not a single authenticated chemical munition was ever recovered
the perfect

fusarium occur naturally in the environment
grow on food supplies and produce toxin   w e a p o n

to accept the chemical-warfare theory of yellow rain
one would have to imagine   an enemy so devious
its chemical weapon is prepared by gathering pollen
predigested by honeybees   which is why not

fact that "bees" defecate | neither proves nor disproves

his theory does not explain the human and animal morbidity and pathology

a matter of degree, speed of onset and number of victims

when an entire village decimated in a very short time

like li h ood

of natural contamination is extremely weak

[Jiangsu] no analysis as to toxicity were performed | totally different picture to that experienced in

not seen fit to attempt to reproduce the experiments that he considers faulty

a s ho uld

be done by any honest scientist from Harvard

Mirocha | in 15 years of testing | detected T-2 only infrequently | at levels no

higher than 50 ppb | don't find these levels in nature

Nelson | no scientific evidence that toxin-producing

fus ari um

occurs naturally in Southeast Asia

Jarvis | unlikely that

the toxins would occur naturally at higher levels in all 3 villages

Hess ettin e |

unlikely that the amounts of toxin found would be produced

naturally | no overgrowth of fungus

Mirocha | no evidence that a pathogenic fusarium

species | host's substrate for synthesis of trichothecene and deposit

it on the leaves

no evidence that fusarium can colonize

inanimate objects (rocks) and produce trichothecenes

No such disease outbreaks attributed to

T-2

| ever been recognized or recorded in Laos

Schiefer producers of trichothecenes exist

in the area | neither naturally

occurring diseases | nor are there any detectable

Rip po n

fusarium has rarely caused human

disease in tropical climates people have been walking

around in these moldy

jun gles

for years haven't had any problems with fusarium

Mirocha | highly improbable

that fusarium could survive a n d

produce the large quantities

N o wic ke |

hard to imagine | that any

one bee

would collect this tremendous diversity of

pol len

to produce high levels of toxins substrate

must be heavily invaded by fungi | would no longer be yellow

| have an off-white color | would be fluffy

or matted rather than powdery

yet to be demonstrate d | will result · in the formation of high concentrations of both Type A · and trichothecen es in nature · B · problem with the bee feces theory is the failure to detect HT-2

abs enc e · of HT-2 toxin | not in accord with a natural · explanation | laboratory cultures of Fusarium spp. · produce HT-2 toxin · no t

b e e n established Fusarium spp. can grow on · fece s · let alone produce secondary metabolites such as mycotoxins | · in the high concentratio ns reported

trich othe cene s · are not produced on unwashed and unsterilized pollen even · under controlled · laboratory conditions | not a good competitor in colonizing organic matter · such a s

pollen and will be outgrown · by more aggressive fungi · under controlled laboratory conditions only one of thirteen · Fusarium spp. isolates collected in Thailand was capable

of · producing trichothecene s | in low yield · presence of polyethylene glycol in a powder · bee feces theory | its genesis · i n sampl e s

collected yellow powder on a Thai village | · unidentified aircraft | two samples that w e r e · positive contaminated with pollen | not too surprising collected during · t h e pollinating season | could have become

cont amin ated · with pollen before | after a yellow rain | · peo ple · collected and turned in anything that w a s · yel low

which is it was perfect

w h y t h e

we ap on · whi c h · si why wase · tth e

perfect · whi ch is why

Enter Dr. Matthew Meselson, scientist at Harvard University, government consultant, specialist in chemical and biological defense, proponent of arms control. Above all, a supporter of the BWC and its pretense of peace.

November 1982. The State Department announced at a press briefing the discovery of pollen in test samples, similar to the kind carried by honeybees.

Early 1983. Meselson took a leaf sample he obtained from one scientist and gave it to another scientist, Dr. Joan Nowicke at the Smithsonian Institution, who discovered on it a variation of spots resembling pollen.

April 1983. Meselson convened a conference in Cambridge, Massachusetts, to discuss yellow rain. There he met botanist Peter Ashton. Together they reached out to a bee expert at Yale University, Dr. Thomas Seeley, who said the spots were simply bee shit. Suddenly, Ashton noticed bee shit in his yard for the first time. Meselson, too, realized bee shit landed on people's cars.

May 31, 1983. Meselson announced at a conference that it was all just shit. No biological weapon here, they claimed. No BWC violation, they headlined.

March 1984. Meselson and Seeley went to Thailand to research Southeast Asian honeybees. They placed paper on the jungle floor, then returned periodically to inspect it. Suddenly, the yellow spots appeared. These bees shit, they argued. Those who lobbied for arms-control could now depict a veneer of peace and the Soviets could claim innocence.

They made the Hmong appear as if we were confused, as if we couldn't tell the difference between what the earth gave and what man made, the difference between shit and death.

The Culpable

When all else fails, you'll indict the bees.

When all else rushes at your awareness
in the stage of sudden beasts,

> you'll second guess
> if it had been the bees.

You'll claim the moonlight betrayed you,
to know and see anything but only with a knife.

When all else relents and you are kneeled for
an answer,

> you'll go back
> to spying on the bees,

censuring their chorus the way you faulted
us into outlaws, caught between

hopeless and hopelessness,
doubting us in the throat of your blame,

saying malice to the grass, saying bees
sired the venom

> that sired our lies that could
> sire another war.

What fate tilted in your favor, counter
the weight back to us.

What fate tilted in your favor,
> counter
> the weight
> back to bees.

Sverdlovsk

In 1979, an anthrax outbreak in the Soviet city of Sverdlovsk led many Western security officials to conclude that the Soviets had been clandestinely developing biological weapons in violation of the 1972 Biological Weapons Convention. . . . [T]he final death toll approached one thousand. . . . The response [the Soviets] took was direct: bad meat caused the Sverdlovsk deaths. . . . Granted clearance to look at a special CIA study of the Sverdlovsk events, and having heard the full brunt of the Soviet story, [Meselson] commented: "I spent many hours looking at classified material. I disagree with the conclusion the [US] government reached. That is all I am allowed to say."

—**Article by Michael D. Gordin,** *Journal of the History of Biology,* **1997**

[Meselson] continues to be convinced that the anthrax outbreak there was of natural origin.   —*The New Yorker,* **February 18, 1991**

You were wrong   about Sverdlovsk
for deceiving   your first story
wrong as you clung   to the wires   of your ego
as to forget night   is a harbor for the past.

Let things come clean in a scandalous
              tornado of shimmering truth.

It turns out   you were wrong
to say the Soviets   had no part
when in fact   they had overthrown
the sea   every moon
steeped in its tides:

I knew about the existence   at this post of a closed
research
center   but I had no information

about what it was doing   specifically . . .
I appealed to the Ministry of Defence . . .

*A large group of military   and KGB people
arrived. They did not inform me   personally of the
results . . .*

        *some of the laboratories were
removed . . .*

        —Public statement by Boris Yeltsin, November 1, 1990

When in fact   it took so little
to make a tale   happen and let soak
with you   what they
would mask.

To build an   accident or
to build   a situation in which
the accident   could be tested.

*. . . technician at the military facility   [failed]
    to close a valve   to the outside,
  enabling a small,   accidental burst   of spores
to
    escape the room through   a small shaft . . .*

And so little   could be asked
to make   the Soviets pay
for all those   lives stolen
in Sverdlovsk.   How does anyone flat
fracture   a confession from
an empire   absolved of
           its reign.

*. . . hard-liner   Reagan ignored   Yellow Rain and
the plight of the Hmong: "In the big picture, SALT
and the
        USSR are far more   important
  than a couple of hundred thousand   Hmongs in an
area
where we don't have   any interest," said an
    anonymous   Reagan   administration
official.*

Had you done accurate by
the ancestors all the names
lost in Sverdlovsk
had you split the rivers open
to let drift their speech.

Coughing out forgeries
in bottomless fields you spared not the terrain
but only the masses
of your own feet.

Malediction

Let this be about a dirt runway
                          tucked inside
            a domain of high grasses,

a season of nectar

        for the deceased
to drink the muscle and medulla
                          of rebirth.

Let this lead to a reckoning of fences
under duskward,

        a swing of your judgment
                  against the will of Gaia.

    Let fall a rage of grace
to caretake the year ahead.

            Let everything speak to the
        privilege of your station,

                    as man,
                    as west,
                    as science,
                    as crooked law,

as man of west in science of crooked laws.

Let this never stop being about your privilege.

        Let this be about
            the muzzle
                  from which you weaponize
                          phantom facts,

danger of your kind to charge
the harmless,

tomb of your decency
        that you and the doom
          will swaddle to your kin.

Never to Have Had Your Song Blessed

The Hmong are a superstitious people prone to believing that spirits cause illness and death. The Hmong were subjected to US aerial herbicide spraying in the '60s. They could have made an association between aircraft and yellow substances to death and illness.

—Paper authored by the US Arms Control and Disarmament Agency, quoting Meselson, with point-by-point rebuttals to his comments on yellow rain, July 2, 1984

That you should venture to go this small

Entertain the bloodnuts to rest humanity
    On a wager with the spirits
    On a psyche to insult the divine

That you have hungered for
    Your own clever existence

Though never to have slept
    In the elderlight of past bones

How does your heritage respond
    To the surge of patterns
    All thundering the same wound

Losing you untied

It is not our fault
    No one has swept their palm to the floor
    No one called up your soul fallen to the land

Not our fault
    No one has fed your tribe

Notes in Rebuttal: What They May Have Known about the Possibility

Testimony of Meselson, Chemical Biological Weapons Hearing before the Committee on Foreign Relations, April 30, 1969

[The beauty is that it won't happen right away. They'll want it to hit you only after the fact. Let you live in the giving of their slow crisis.]

. . . biological agents take some time before their effect is manifested. . . . [O]ne and a few days. . . . [B]ecause of that delay, they are not generally considered for tactical use on the battlefield, but rather for strategic use.

[Strategic as in covert. As in to pre-weaken. As in pre-attack before the actual attack. As in post-promise. As in post-attack should the actual attack fail to purge a populace.]

The most generally considered mode of attack . . . would be the release of an aerosol cloud, by planes or drones. . . . [P]articles from the aerosol mist must generally lodge in the deep recesses of the lungs. . . . The pulmonary form of a disease, that is, the form which strikes first in the lungs, is generally more severe . . .

[As if to speak of a thing is what brings the thing into existence.

As if to speak of a thing means the thing might already exist.]

I certainly agree that you might kill an enormous fraction of the population with a biological weapon. I also believe, however, that as strategic weapons go, these are ridiculous weapons . . .

[Ridiculous is to downplay the severity.]

. . . ridiculous because they in no way would reduce the ability of the country attacked to retaliate with nuclear missiles . . .

[But consider: (1) the attack disguised as a naturally occurring phenomenon, (2) the toxin engineered to degrade quickly, in which case, (3) cause of death attributed to natural phenomenon, leading to (4) no retaliation.]

. . . and they also might not work.

[RDTE. Research Development Testing and Evaluation.]

These weapons, in my opinion, hold certain advantages for poor countries, small countries, who might not have nuclear weapons—but not for nuclear powers.

[To subdue the other by offensive means. Then blame it on a health scare. Call it a natural phenomenon. Say it's just the weather. Then wash your hands clean.]

Nobody can say today whether an anthrax bomb would work or not work.

[Ten years later, Sverdlovsk worked.]

. . . it may well be possible to devise weapons containing far more poisonous materials, perhaps toxins or related substances.

[Deoxynivalenol. Nivalenol. T-2. HT-2. Diacetoxyscirpenol.]

Senator Case: Some of the things you have said suggest it would be a lot better to have this in reserve as a retaliatory weapon . . .

Meselson: The important thing is to look at it through the lens of preventing the use of these weapons, and it may be that through that lens you need to prepare certain retaliatory forces.

[Hypocrisy of deterrence. To rationalize the need for weapons. On the basis:
         it discourages other nations.

       They say. Weapons are created. To deter their own use. To make null their own necessity.]

[Monster yourself.

    Exert evil to dissuade evil
in others.]

[Preventative measures. As motive to conquer.]

[As initiation of conflict.]

[As manifestation of war.]

All of a Sudden, Yellow Spots

Meselson, remembering that the Museum of Comparative Zoology [in Cambridge, Massachusetts] had a nest of honeybees on its roof. . . . Sure enough, he found a number of yellow spots on the windows of several cars.

The research facilities at the Smithsonian's Museum of Natural History include a working beehive on the roof, and several days later, when Meselson went to Washington, he and Nowicke looked around the museum's lot and discovered that Nowicke's own car, a Volkswagen station wagon, was covered with yellow spots. —**The New Yorker, February 11, 1991**

How is it you had never noticed before?

Science: does it teach you
                    to invent the answers you seek?

        Finagle the aftermath in your favor?

                Slanted objectivity. Partial to your politics.

And the commotion of yellow rain
                    conjunct with your decision to
        realize the existence
                        of yellow spots and then
                declare the droppings
                                of bees   ?
                                    ?
                    ?
                        ?

All this while.

            Why do you grasp it
                    now? Does this timing
                feel too tampered? Does this
                            make me ask?
                    ?
                        ?   ?
            ?   ?
                        ?

Recantation for the Quieting

Stand and die in our stead,
straggling toward daybreak

as organisms hounded by the
undead. Highlands out of

reach, remote from first steps
as almighty ether. A forlorn

river to stash the remnant
flesh of your war. When after

we've offered our side of the
reckoning to then be dressed

inside a snitch, who of you
will save us from the pyre?

To suppose our stake had been
removed, we were wrong to

say anything. We take back
the water of our tones, flip

the words from under the loyalty
of our tongue. While we

live in carnage of the honesty
we take back, we live at all.

Il/Logic, Fully Unvetted: A Makeshift Analysis of the Behavior of Southeast Asian Honeybees

1. Migration of Bees: Resource Depletion, Seasonal Considerations

[A. florea and A. andreniformis] in Thailand . . . abscond in response to increased exposure to heat/sunlight and during dearth . . .

Absconding/migrations by thousands of colonies of A. dorsata coincide with the monsoon, which determines the dry and rainy seasons, hence the onset of resource depletion . . .

The attacks occurred all throughout the year, although there were reduced numbers of attacks in Southeast Asia during the wet season.

Bees abscond due to → dearth, heat, sunlight → indicating DRY season

Most of the attacks happened during the DRY season
↓
But if the bees had already absconded during the DRY season
↓
Then what was causing the attacks?

2. Elevation Considerations

. . . colonies typically live in lofty communal nest sites . . . at relatively high elevation . . . during the dry season. . . . As forage decreases toward the end of the season, colonies abandon their combs and migrate to lower elevations, establishing new nests there for the mass flowering of the monsoon season.

Bees are at high elevation → during the DRY season
Bees change to low elevation → as WET season approaches

The Hmong lived primarily at high elevation

↓

If bees moved to lower elevation during the WET season

↓

Why were there still

↓

Scattered attacks reported during the WET season?

↓

In places of higher elevation?

3. Migration of Bees: Distance/Time Traveled

*After occupying a nest site for several months, all or most colonies
abscond and travel to an alternative site, which may be 200 km
away . . .*

*A. dorsata very evidently move considerable distances in the course
of migration. . . . [S]warms may take as much as a month to reach
their final destination . . . along the way they frequently stop.*

Vast distances of 200 km +
Month-long duration of bee movement +
Bee feces showers +
Hmong standing/running underneath feces showers +
Exact timing ≈
Not entirely impossible, but is most
=
Unlikely

4. Migration of Bees: Stopover Sites/Bivouacs

*A. dorsata bivouacs [stopover sites during migration] found over
two consecutive monsoon seasons congregated in and around a
riverside mango grove in northern Thailand.*

Vast distances of 200 km +

Month-long duration of bee movement +

Bee bivouacking along the way +

Bee feces showers +

Hmong standing/running underneath feces showers +

Exact timing =

Too many poorly understood and scantily vetted variables

≠

Anything definitive

5. Migration of Bees: Site Fidelity

. . . same [bivouac] site was occupied in consecutive years, and knowledgeable field workers report that groups of giant honey bees gather there annually . . . I speculate that they have used trees on the site of the Mae Hong Son BCSS [bivouac congregation stopover site] for millennia.

. . . migrating A. dorsata swarms are astonishingly faithful to their nest sites. . . . They may even return to the same eave or branch. It is not known how they do this, but the mechanism is probably related to chemical signatures left by the departing swarm and recognized by the returning swarm.

Bees remain loyal to former nest sites

↓

Returning to them year after year, decade after decade

↓

If it had been the bees

↓

One should be able to visit an attack site today

↓

Look up in the trees, branches

↓

Find nests and hives within reasonable proximity

=

Find the bees

+

If no nests?

=

No bees

6. Migration of Bees: Tree Preferences

Bivouacs favored mango trees more. . . . Doubtless some tree species are more desirable than others. For example, though the BCSS was lined with tall Eucalyptus trees, I never saw a bivouac in this smooth-barked species, to which it may be difficult for bivouacs to cling. No clusters utilized nearby, numerous pomelo trees. Factors such as shade and angle of tree branches may be important . . .

Bees prefer particular species of trees

↓

What kind of tree species grew where the attacks happened?

7. Periodic Mass Flights: Distance to Nest Site

In Nepal we also found (in April 1996) enormous amounts of yellow spots . . . accumulated at a distance of 30 m from the nests of A. dorsata.

Which could mean

↓↓↓

If bees were the culprit

↓

Nests should be within vicinity =
Attack sites

8. Periodic Mass Flights: Frequency

Colonies of A. dorsata perform varying numbers of short, daily periodic mass flights (PMFs) ranging in number from zero to six . . .

Even in the warmest monsoon month in Delhi (in July 1984 at 48 degrees Celsius and high humidity rate) massed flight behavior happened periodically and the intensity and duration was similar to that in November.

. . . defecation is another aspect of mass flight.

Mass flight
↓
On a regular, daily basis
↓
To defecate, among other reasons
↓
[*A. dorsata* in other parts of Asia → mass flights
even during the WET season → just as much as during the DRY season]
↓
So if bees defecate year round on constant, regular basis
↓
Reports of yellow rain attacks should have also happened year round
↓
On constant, regular basis
↓
But they did not

Bees actively defecating +
Even during the WET season ≠
Consistent, steady reports of attacks every month of every year
≠
Death by naturally occurring phenomenon
≠
The bees

Prayer to the Redwood

Senescent and dwelling
      In your tower with sorrel

    For shoes, I come to you fleshed
With intention,

A muted engine
        Dismantled at your coastal throne,

   In doubt and daring
Intuit from you:

        Tell me if you've
    Heard of the Apis dorsata *and I*
       Will affirm
    What I know of its innocence.

    Take this confession to your
Wildlife, mahogany limbs

Grasping the upper
      Avenues of your genius memory

       As readily there a
Nursery for hemlock and new firs.

   How would you have guarded your pine?
These sudden flecks, you would have

Known its taste as factory-born far from organic consent,
      You would have deemed its

         False footprint.
   Here in your globe's

Fluent echo, you exhale the words:
> Stockpile, degrade, human subjects.

I make sentient
My palm over your bark of suede,

> Dense as it were to defy
A passing inferno.

> Stockpile, degrade, human subjects.
No secret must ever be singed of your knowing.

Allied with the Bees

These people have been living in these areas for all their life but they have never heard or experienced something like this before. Bees and honey are part of their life; they and their ancestors have traded honey for salt, clothes, and other goods for hundreds of years.

—Letter to the Editor by S. Yang, Long Beach, April 6, 1984

Tell them, child, we have hiked
These hills without shoes, long
Enough to hunt alongside the bees,

    Memorizing the bend, pulse
    Of their voices when they
    Go dream inside the trees.

We have been crowned with
Syrup of their toils so that our
Syntax might awaken to know

    Its full range, compassed to
    The North, pristine as a nomadic
    Butterfly. Tell them, daughter,

We watched as they buried their
Queen, folding her into cashmere
Of her wings before swarming

    The body toward a fire of stars.
    And for days, the forest keened
    A shadow lullaby. And for nights,

We listened for the bees only
To uncover the hurried hush of our
Own stranded feet, falling forgotten

As collateral beings. Tell them,
Me ntxhais, we are not misled in
Our anguish, what happened

To the bees also happened to us.

Composition 4

abundance of pollen
its presence suggested that yellow rain has a natural origin

best of our knowledge
all the samples of the yellow material examined under the microscope have, without exception, been found to consist primarily of pollen

to discuss the evidence
Stewart Schwartzstein of the Institute for Foreign Policy Analysis
one of us (Meselson) assembled a conference in Cambridge, Mass

the feces
take the form of small, yellow, pollen-filled spots that dry to a powder

yellow rain
an accurate description of the fecal droppings of honeybees

plant taxa
identified from the pollen in yellow rain are common in Southeast Asia

more vigorous test program
large-scale field tests should be conducted to determine the effectiveness of specific BW agents under operational conditions

most attractive and profitable uses is in the field of covert operations

special agents or guerilla forces operating behind enemy lines to place small quantities of BW agents accurately where they could be most effective

distinction between this type of BW and naturally occurring outbreaks is most difficult

no two spots
have the same mixture
of pollen types

such diversity
in the composition
of the pollen from
spot to spot is
characteristic of
honeybee feces, but it
would not be
expected from a
manmade mixture

indeed gathered by
Southeast Asian
honeybees

capability for producing
mycotoxin considered very
important by FDA

a proposal would be looked
upon with favor

report is a translation from Russian

Having solved the specific technical problems of developing and producing
biological weapons, the Americans are moving on to the next stage in
mastering them -- training the troops and bringing them up to a state of
constant combat readiness

the biological
aerosol, which can spread over a large area

wide use in operations against partisans based in areas (mountains, swamps)
that are difficult for troops

assessing the meteorological factors and terrain
conditions

employing pathogens through infected insects

biological warfare
means by using missiles

observations
showed showers of honeybee
feces do indeed
occur in the Tropics
of Southeast Asia

closely resemble
the showers and spots said to be
caused by yellow rain

effective Soviet and client state control over access to the regions and the rapid degradation of the agents after dissemination must have argued strongly against the likelihood that outsiders would acquire persuasive evidence of the violation

They may well have calculated that they and their allies could successfully counter or deny charges that chemical weapons had been used, recognizing that it would be as difficult to compile incontrovertible evidence from Southeast Asia and Afghanistan

remote areas as providing unique opportunities for the operational testing and evaluation of chemical weapons under various tactical conditions

| 87TH CONGRESS 2d Session | HOUSE OF REPRESENTATIVES | REPORT No. 1477 |

IMPORTATION OF HONEY BEES

H.R. 8050

MARCH 22, 1962.—Committed to the Committee of the Whole House on the State of the Union and ordered to be printed

Until recently it was believed that *Apis mellifera* was the only species of honey bees which carried the acarine mite, which is responsible for acarine disease, the most serious single disease affecting honey bees. Recently, however, an infestation of these mites was found on another species of honey bees which had been imported into the United States for use at the Beltsville Experiment Station.

to assure protection of honey bees in the United States from this disease, the importation of adults of all species of honey bees must be prohibited, except for experimental purposes under controlled conditions. experimental purposes

137

hypothesis
yellow rain is the feces of Asian honeybees

SUBJECT: Meeting With COL Robinson, HQDA DCSOPS on 9 July 82

1. Purpose and Activity Visited:

_____ visited COL (P) Bobby Robinson, Deputy Director, Nuclear and Chemical Directorate, DCSOPS, HQDA at the Pentagon on 9 July 1982. The purpose of the meeting was to acquaint COL Robinson with the scope of LSB CBW intelligence activities

       B. COL Robinson highlighted the US Army's increasing interest in CW.

       (1) The level of Army emphasis is reflected in the resources allocated to the CW mission. The budget has increased from 60 million dollars to over six billion dollars for offensive CW and defensive BCW related activities over the POM years (five year program).

(2) Stockages of chemical defensive equipment are being increased.

status of the principal CW R&D laboratory, Chemical Systems Laboratory, has been increased

increased funding and involvement of all major laboratories.

binary chemical munitions been partially funded.

expanded research and development

Dr. Matthew Meselson, who was the first to tell me about Jerry Daniels' death, called me this past spring (1987) to again deliver bad tidings

General Robinson, a colonel at the time Bohica took place and one of the persons I had originally called to verify the mission, had allegedly committed suicide

was at that time Commander of the Pine Bluff Arsenal for Chemical and Biological Warfare

second

main figure connected with the mission to die mysteriously

during '81 Robinson was working on something very sensitive with a chemical warfare problem in Indochina

138

I choose what belongs to earth. I call for a reckoning of time. I follow what was left behind, fog of tropic lineage layered among the debris of old songs. I break the pages and let the bees fly out.

Noxious

No is the mind of the orphaned storm,
    Gravity of skin falling off in great sheets.

They built this stealth weather wrought from faux organs
      Without a cloud to its breath.

      What they built was a winter in which to leave me.

No is the yellow wing, rainspots
    On banana leaves as fingerprints of the dead.

It is the wish to hunt ice when the blood learns
    The meaning of never.

It is the rise inside
A rooster's crow, pretense of arms

     From a ragged shape made unwhole.

     The face is a mechanical cloth
    Tethered to the evocation of daylight.

     They stockpile the hours in
         Beds of the missing,
In shattered vials gathered by the witnessing moon.

Orderly Wrap-Up of CBW Investigation

There will be no wrap-up press releases; Washington has developed press guidance for use on an if-asked basis. . . . Please inform Washington if the team is experiencing any problems in its wrap-up procedures. We would also appreciate information on RTG [Royal Thai Government] reaction to the disestablishment of the team. —**Cable from the Secretary of State to the US Embassy, Bangkok, October 25, 1986**

Expect no farewells to mark this pageant of fiasco

No lanterns or recollections of the famished

No sprig of a conifer free from redaction

Nor footnotes to crop a new village

There will be no parade to crawl alongside tigers

Anyone who leaves behind their spirit

Anyone who whistles in the night

Any talk of the enemy's ear

There will be no sediment of our aura to find

No closure extending from a bridge

Blot every bee every memo every cable

Blot every map every report every illness

Shred it all   Misfiled and elapsed

Nested and re-rendered   Utensil of our fist

        Shred it all   Sullied and blank

We demand for orderly emptiness to remain

Of the Ash

One more stint
Of soaring turns
The starling marvels
Nightward.

        One circus of
        Alloyed men as
        Spectators whose
        Every pin-song

                And wick is
                Gritted. When
                There are alarms
                To outlast

All the others,
They'll know
That homeland
Is the heart's name

        For halcyon. They'll
        Filter a nightmare
        As the middle of all
        Waiting for mold

                That grows inside
                Their dreams.
                Summoned by
                Mint. They sob for

Brightness that
Harpoons the
Migrating drowse,
How it downs

Into their tincture
Of awareness.
What they know
Of experience—

Clandestine is to
Let oneself be
Imagined by the
Dust. If the reason

To leave had
Been falling,
They'll die deprived
Of a roof to their

Name, without
Nacre to ask if
There had been
No war to lose.

Vigil for the Missing

On my most nocturnal days, the icebergs
Stop listening to me. They shift their sails

Away from my breathing. They tell me I am
Not made of mirrors but from a wolf that slept

In a grave and gave birth to a sunrise. She is
The fruit that formed me, the dense coat of silk

Shadowing me out of the ice. Sometimes I
Dream in the voice of another empire, and

I see its feet slink through the crosshairs,
Clipping around shells and splinters of trapped

Fires. Its ballroom caves ripple out murmurings
Of the lost ones, despair mottling the dark as

Small searchlights. Lost Ones, who linger
Through a solar rage, I know your pain lives

Cardinal. Love spills from your hallucinations.
Once, a child whispered into me: such sorrow

Can only be followed by a decade of snow.
I crawled into the sky and wept a puddle

Of sweet laurel until I bled at the ankles, until
Grandmother called: *come in from the winter.*

The Shaman Asks about Yellow Rain

Did the airplane knife the sky? Or did it arrive,
    Still and unruffled
    As a mass grave?

Did it drone a foreign talk, tune of a soggy
    Friendship, or maybe
    It was lit from

An acquainted hum? Did you look up to earth's
    Tinted azure for one
    Terrific minute?

What of the power, as if sand had been thrown
    In your face, as if innards
    Had been scheming

To leave you. How long before your flesh slipped off?
    Did you hear distant
    Men chatter of their

Armless nation, hoarding amputated limbs? Maybe
    The babbling entered in reverse,
    A camouflaged back

Turned to you, the deletion of your death
    As more than collateral,
    Erasure of these toxins

To prevent spilling of the globe's intestines.
    Did you locate your way
    To the hills of lineage

Without a guidesong to keep pace, without
    A ground to sleep you?
    How many decades

Before you landed at the heirloom shore, jacketed
      Within flames of beige?
      Did you tell them of the

Western rains, a speckled land that slipped into
      A canal and then
      Broke into downpour?

Let them know. Let the ancient ones keen their oath
      Lyrics. Let them scrape each leaf,
      Each spoiled bark,

Pieces of corroded lint, every spell of hemorrhaging.
      Let them one day utter
      The narrative uncloaked.

Refugee, Walking Is the Most Human of All

So long to the papaya   kingdoms
      Of olden mothers,

        The shepherdess igniting
  Peels of bergamot.

    Grief of chalk
      Scribbles the form of an
            Archangel.

        Consider   a pillow of mortars,
  How the rubble of hair

Weighs dense together
      With the pedestrian heft

  Of never coming back.

Home is a sleeping whale.

      Consider an armor
Of feathers, not to buffer   the body from shelling,

  But to be hoisted
As a skyless meteor fleeing for

        An elsewhere chance
           To land.

You will come back
To rescue your footsteps.

      Towels spread on a road
As if forming: timeline
        Of cotton against

A pillared topography.

But this, the clap of hands in crisis
    Shoveling out evacuees.

        Empty your opera
           In the howling of the sea.

Revolt of Bees

Recently, scientists have exploited the honey bees' exceptional sense of smell . . .
trained bees to detect the scent of various explosive materials. . . . [R]esearchers
are exploring genetic and physiological differences between bees. . . . Ideally,
a superior bee could be developed through genetic engineering. . . . Plans also
include integrating very small fluidic devices to carry chemicals that could be
delivered through the cyborgs' sting. Ultimately, DARPA hopes to "hack into
the insects' own natural senses, allowing the remote-control operator to look
out of the insects own eyes, instead of attaching a video camera for it to carry."

—Research paper by Lois Delaney, submitted in partial fulfillment
for the degree of Master of Military Studies, US Marine Corps,
Marine Corps University, March 30, 2011

Achieve us into your   creatured machine
So that we may shrine   before you
                          As immortal

This is how   you love us   in your illness
                          Of benevolence

Your mind a canister   for vanity
   By merging   our wings with steel

You nourish us with a need   to war with you

                    We will show you
         The plague   you've made of us

Butchery of our eyes   no longer in our
Belonging

               As you condition us with
                          A diet of bombs
     No more
To return   the bounty of your spring

But only to murder   your harvest
Rupture your remembrance
Of nectar

Clover
Goldenrod
Lantana
Thyme

Retribution is the devil
Begging to be   pardoned

Is the devil always homesick   is the devil

Dangling   from a situation
Of blade

Clingstone peach   almond   plum

We will raise a scorching
On your tongue   so bloomed and medieval

Your sense   of sweetened
Will cease to begin

Composition 5

PRO ARMS

ANTI ARMS

The chemical-weapons lobby was given a significant boost late in 1979, when the State Department released documents relaying reports of interviews with refugees concerning lethal chemical attacks...
The New Yorker, 2/11/91

—to shift the onus for the lack of progress in CW arms control from the US to the USSR.

— to make the Soviets pay an appropriate political price for these activities;

-- to reduce Soviet credibility

...chemical-weapons attacks in Southeast Asia was being used to pressure Congress to begin funding production of a 155-mm. nerve-gas binary artillery shell.
The New Yorker, 2/11/91

...would be most likely to be chemical munitions policies and programs.

a Soviet chemical threat would drive U.S. lethal chemical munitions policies and programs.

scientists became convinced that the scientific process itself, in pursuit of its Cold War objectives, was covering up or distorting scientific data and abusing the scientific process... *The New Yorker, 2/11/91*

Dr. Meselson led a well publish ed and publicized crusade to show that the accounts of Yellow Rain by the Hmong were not chemical/toxin attacks, but just the natural cleansing flights of bees.
Katz Dissertation, 2005

...many people in the defense establishment felt that in the interim the Soviet Union had been b u i l d i n g toward an offensive chemical-weapons capabili t y .
The New Yorker, 2/18/91

[Meselson] said, "...you must remember that we are embarking on some of the most important arms-control negotiations in history, and we cannot undercut them."
The New Yorker, 2/18/91

Meselson helped create the Biological Weapons Convention and was committed to proving that chemical and biological weapons were not being used by the Soviet Union (or any other nation), as that would have meant a violation and failure of the treaty.
Katz Dissertation, 2005

155

...Schiefer put to rest the complaint made by some scientists that trichothecenes are not toxic enough to cause the severe symptoms and lethality described by survivors of yellow rain attacks.

Declassified Cables Add to Doubts About U.S. Disclosures on 'Yellow Rain'

mixture of three different types of trichothecenes (T-2, DAS and DON)

"the cocktail was absolutely killing within 24 hours and by 48 hours every animal {mice and rats} from the whole group was dead." *WSJ,* 5/30/84

Mr. Meselson said that he now generally accepts the work of Canadian toxicologist Bruno Schiefer showing that trichothecene mycotoxins don't occur naturally in Southeast Asia – at least not to any significant extent that might cause a health problem. *WSJ,* 9/6/85

The cables from Southeast Asia, the critics say, now cast doubt on the hundreds of interviews with supposed witnesses. They show, for example, that one refugee who said he had seen an attack "with his own eyes" changed his account when reinterviewed by the American team to say he had simply heard of the attack from others.

Dr. Meselson said, "There is no respectable case left for the Administration's accusation of toxin warfare." *NYT,* 8/31/87

FOLLOW-UP ANALYSIS: ONLY WASHINGTON, HOWEVER, WILL BE IN A POSITION TO TELL THE WORLD WHAT, IF ANYTHING, THE COLLECTED EVIDENCE MEANS.

...Meselson proposes that as illiterate indigenous people, they just didn't understand what was happening to them, and they were confusing bee pollen and naturally occurring disease with chemical/toxin weapons attacks. *Katz Dissertation, 2005*

The Department of Defense wants to modernize the stockpile with binary munitions which it says would provide advantages in production, safety, transportation, handling, storage, and disposal. In 1986, Congress approved the manufacture of both weapons [155-mm. binary artillery shells and binary chemical bomb known as Bigeye] but stipulated that it would not begin before October 1, 1987. The United States again began producing chemical weapons in December of 1987. *The New Yorker, 2/18/91*

The Department of Defense believes the existing U.S. stockpile of chemical munitions is inadequate and does not constitute a credible deterrent.

...alle gatio n s height ened the existing atmosp here of con f r o n t ation between the two super powers and d a r k e n ed the outlook for progress in the arms-control negotiations... *The New Yorker, 2/18/91*

yellow rain continued to be portrayed as a serious impediment to fruitful negotiations between the United States and the Soviet Union on chemical disarmament. *The New Yorker, 2/18/91*

...a bitter controversy that cast a persistent shadow over arms-control negotiations between the two great powers. *The New Yorker, 2/11/91*

PRO ARMS

Both the United States and the Soviet Union have defense policies that call for stockpiling chemical munitions to deter the Soviet Union from starting a chemical war. Should deterrence fail, the stockpile would be used to retaliate against a chemical attack.

The United States maintains a stockpile of chemical munitions to deter other nations from using chemical munitions against U.S. Armed Forces or its allies. If deterrence fails, the stockpile is to provide the option of retaliating.

effective deterrent of the use of CW is required to redress the present imbalance in US vs. Soviet capabilities and to enable the US to negotiate from a strengthened position to Current US Planning calls for extensive modernization of our CW capabilities as a deterrent against Soviet CW use.

When the biological weapons Convention (BWC) was negotiated in 1972, the US recognized that it any event, it was inadequately verifiable and that, in were not acceptable to the Soviets. However, verification measures US felt such an agreement to be in the national interest.

the questionable military utility of biological weapons was thought to make violations unlikely

ANTI ARMS

Focus at the UNGA on verification and compliance questions can allow the US both to embarrass the Soviets and to begin expounding a principled position on these issues which we can carry into other arms control fora.

The 'Bee Feces' Theory Undone

Harvard biochemist Matthew Meselson now admits that his original "bee feces" theory of Southeast Asian yellow rain deaths..."is not very attractive anymore."

Mycotoxins: The Scientific Battlefield

The Embarrassment of Yellow Rain:

The Editorial Notebook:

evidence grows that the gathered "yellow rain" is no weapon but almost certainly the pollen-laden excrement of bees

Ms. Cohen said that the "onus" was on those who claim that the mycotoxins found in yellow rain are a natural phenomenon to find bee pollen in Southeast Asia contaminated with trichothecenes. She concluded that this was unlikely because a mycotoxin contamination of the food chain in Southeast Asia would be "a slow moving pheno menon and very widespread illness. In short, the whole population in the area would fall ill and you would find the contamination in the blood and tissues of the whole population. "This is not what has occurred," she said. *WSJ, 5/30/84*

samples of bee feces he and a colleague brought back from a celebrated expedition to a Thailand jungle last year show no traces of mycotoxins that are widely believed to have killed thousands... *WSJ, 9/6/85*

with out the "smok i n g gun"...remains just a hypothesis.

embarrassingly unproved *NYT, 11/28/83*

a comp licated blend of fact and fiction *The New Yorker, 2/18/91*

I guarantee that the Hmong are some of the best storytellers on earth. They can make up stories faster than you and I can write them down. *The New Yorker, 2/18/91*

It was all in the trajectory of things. The simple consequence of an event, one move in the wrong direction turned the situation futile.

If the State Department had never uttered the word—

If Seagrave had waited—

If Haig had not been so hasty—

If the BWC had included—

If the US government had more fully—

If they had been more diligent in the—

And if there had been no war—

No US intrusion into—

No colonizing of—

I can't stop mourning the what-ifs.

I inherited yellow rain as I also inherited the lost. When my parents recalled what they knew about yellow rain, they did not speak of bees. Only in whispers did the elders say anything about the rain and those who fell beneath it, names and faces left to the mountain, spirits still searching under the leaves.

Burn Copies

24 September 71

Mr. Dan Arnold

Attached for your information are burned
25X1 copies of ▉▉▉▉▉▉▉▉▉▉▉▉ These
are the only copies outside my private file.
If you wish to retain them, please do so in a
secure place. If not, please destroy them.

George A. Carver, Jr.
Special Assistant for Vietnamese Affairs

Attachment

162

Diary Notes from Meeting on September 13, 1983

Source: Leader of the Ban Phu Hae Village Defense Forces under Lao People's Democratic Republic (LPDR) authorities who regularly attended propaganda meetings with Pathet Lao/Vietnam (PL/VN) officials.

—**Cable from the US Embassy, Bangkok, to the Secretary of State, October 31, 1983**

At which point the flora
gave way to temples

of wild yams   At each turn
into rotted fruit came
ragged   shelves of

cassava for a generation
unfed

A) Vang Pao would not be returning to Laos.

A longitude collapsing five
dimensions before the hungered ones

find a way back   As if to map
a fragile breed   End to righteousness

In view of their bragging
lessons   Let the record abandon

B) Laos is under PL/VN Soviet control.

They tell you a sensation
that has nagged   A prized nemesis

glowing under a victory
of disease   All your fears to be

resolved in   outer space

C) The United States was launching airborne chemical attacks against Hmong villagers, but that nobody should worry as the Soviets had a space station which could combat this menace.

Theirs   is a forged provenance

       a desecrated   lease
to abide as they   intend

D) The Soviets were rulers of the world.

Reminders of   a pestering logic
     as to repeat their own
               reflection

As to copyright the work of blood

E) The United States had killed 3,000 Hmong in airborne gas/chemical attacks since 1975.

How much deeper   higher this metric
      might go

         The United States
   The   United States
    The United   States

Could have been   United
               States

Layers upon layers upon
   layers of   verity

      bombarding   your chest

For as Long as a Mountain Can Ascend

Newspaper article by Neil Kelly, Australian correspondent, titled "Meos lose homes in the mountains." —**Carried in the** *Bangkok Post*, **October 12, 1978**

30,000 are hunting Hmong down from the mountains.

Hazards forcing Hmong to the lowlands, scatter Hmong

To the plains. In this outreach of murder they call repression

Campaign, mass scourge of bullied integration. Half of Hmong

Already dead or gone, more of Hmong decisive to make a run

As those who fled at September's end when 1,000 crossed

Mekong, over and above clasping stalks of bamboo, 100,000

More believed to be on the move, sneaking near the enemy's

South. Not as the first war of Indochina, some Hmong took

Arms with Viet Minh at Dien Bien Phu, others alongside Vang

Pao trudged over peaks, futile to reach the defeated fort of

Colonial French. Decades now slipped and Vang Pao has fled

And what remains of his troops in this unanswered war, to stay

Notified of death having ambushed Soviet advisers near Vientiane

Last May. What relics of his troops, their backbones parched from

Grief: men over 45, boys under 16, some less than 10 years too

Young to come down from the mountain, to wander eternal

Refugeless as Hmong through thickets lit without stars, in havoc

And full heartbreak to come down from the mountain.

165

Subject: ROI

. . . US operations in Laos . . . the total cost was less than $500 million per year, including AID, MASF, ■■■ *and the bombing. In all this, we were not losing a single American, and we were killing over thirty North Vietnamese a day. $500 million was what one US division cost us in South Vietnam. In Laos, the same sum enabled us to tie down two North Vietnamese divisions, numerous Binh Tram, plus many trucks and anti-aircraft artillery sites. We were getting a bigger bang for a buck in Laos than anywhere else.*

—Memorandum of conversation, Ambassador Godley's comments to Kissinger on developments in Laos, July 23, 1970

In the name
Of convenience, haggle-free

Exploits into martyred hills, of pawning
Continents as often as highway vintage, in honor

Of dishonest bargains, quality perspiration delivered for free,
In lieu of a more expensive heartbeat, in lieu of two elbows for five

Fires, hollow lineage for erasure, in lieu of one populace borrowed
By the other to be fed generic pennies and a currency of grain.

In duty of as much for as little as bundled together NGOs
With the bombing for less than $500 million for

Laos and her kingdom.

       In all this   not a single American

  In all this   vote of the   unfertile harvest

In all this   incisions to the land   by a slaughterer of plants

   In all this   in lieu of US lives   honor of perjury

Pitted words   in recognition of breached neutrality

In face of contrary   ethics by way of   proxy boots

A Hmong   life

In lieu of a US life
A Hmong life

That if not for a cheap need
To scheme toward peace   If not

For the looted work of men in
Limbo   If such war had not come

To pass   We'd have no fret for
Speckled leaves   No fuss to be

A face in your court of bees nor
Dumped as falsehoods under your

Perverted reckoning   If there
Had been no war   If no war had

Come to pass   If from heaven's
Spine had fallen a concert of sirens

A flockless breeze in lullaby for
The dead   If war had not come and

Home was still ours and billboard
Your patriot lies and no ruined rain

Chasing you to capitulate an outcome
That had never been yours to give

How Far for the Small Ones

Babies get lost in war

> *Pale Hmong woman 26 yr. old delivered a live female infant | before crossing the Mekong River on 10 January, 1983*

No hours to rehearse the act of leaving, no house to repeat escape

> *Picked up their children and ran up into the surrounding hills | fled so quickly | unable to take any livestock*

Then the small feet pattering all its best, trying every hardest

> *Five children were not quick enough | later when the men went back to look | found the children had been shot*

Changing bodies, influx bodies, bodies with bellies, bodies happening in the middle of war

> *Two families remained on the Laos side at Ban Ka | one of the women was near term*

In a cycle in the middle of war

> *Woman claimed to be a victim | June 1978 attack | normal menstrual cycle since the attack*

Under the cover of mother, under the cover of sister, under the cover of great aunt, under grandmother's arm

> *Women would hear an aircraft | gather up the children | run under cover | stay sometimes for half the day*

Leave the wild behind

Twice she saw dead birds | wanted to cook them | men told the women only to cook what they had killed

Little portrait of wishes for every newborn that survives a war, babies of the trapped year

A 22-year-old Hmong woman | 1979 attack near Long Tieng | delivered a normal baby | conceived shortly after the gas attack

In the year of tempted exit, in the year of petrol fevers, in the year of permutation

They could see their village burning
They could see their village burning after they ran
They could see their village burning after they ran into the forest

Gestation lessons on the *known effects of mycotoxins,* on the odds of the unborn, on wheat of the unknown will

Could the toxin produce fetal abnormalities | function | abortifacient or be carcinogenic

Comes the will of the quietest rebel

A US citizen working at Ban Vinai | obtained a two-month-old fetus aborted by a Hmong woman | claims to have been victim of approximately ten chemical attacks

Enters a renouncer of the root for honey of the cause

Provided the fetus | stipulation that it be transmitted for analysis

Enters one footprint in the earth to reservoir as a small pond

Monument

What is the name for an antelope
    who grazes inside a dream

  then vanishes into the
               nebula's brush.

        What is the face
for refurbishing grammar

     at each comma's lip.
      Whose identity never

remembers the shape of beige.
  What is the word

       for how to conjure
   the sigh of a line, hushed

  beneath the flap of a thousand
shifting plumes.

What is the body of a
     garden where a crescent

      despairs, drifts beneath
  the melt of amber.

The season is always growing
out its hooves.

       One cradlesong
  of your leaving is not larger

  than the forest of your arrival.
To make you a noun forever.

     A loss of you
cannot be equal to the loss of you.

Sorrowed

Lark me from this weathering
Into the petrichor after a hailstorm.

There is symmetry in the water
Like I have never seen, peel of

Hydrangea like I have never felt,
Halos sharpened from the taste

Of hexagons. Next to your eyes
In the marrow of this fog into each

Particle of our outcome, I grieve
For the countries flaming in our

Lungs after decades of air forsaken.
I don't want to leave these

Compilations of night, onesome
Even with you as of rain fitted for

Lips undulating toward a smile.
Now this time it loved back, a fruited

Transmuting of my courage into
Smoke and then I heard it to be you:

The sun-swallowed howl of your
Cobra's heart owning its kingdom.

It was never about finding out what actually happened to the Hmong.

Something happened in that jungle. Something still happening. The truth does not offer itself in this life, but here a truth is surfacing.

I circle. I pour into the rains. And I will chase them down until the seasons dry out and the clouds unfold before me the light of a new storm.

Manifesto of a Drum

Predator I've become
        For a truth and fainted tower

      If it means when I turn to cut
        The ache in my spine

           Instead   I find your bitter teeth

Melt your crown
To amend a bayonet for my seeking

    Trophy yourself   Purveyor of peace
          Fathering out schemes

     Post-eagle
Partisan arms

       Doldrums of the fatigued
           No filament for retreat

Even with my sight sealed
  My back turned

       I am not without mystic voltage
          Nor a battalion of the dead

             Never distant
       From the mantle of my kin

*

Billowed
and glinted
as a fixture
into
fluttering   In
                  flight
                  lung
                  vertigos   Etheric mage of
                                      the molecular
                                      dream
                                                        A candescent
                                                    garden aglow   from
                                  Lapis   precipitation to wall
                                  lazuli
                                  rising
                                  to my
                                  sea
            Self-chariot in a
            cyclone of ink
                  Carry me as I have carried you

                                          Show me where to look
                                          as I have shown you
                                          through the burning of
Show   *joss and its divination*
me how
jaded the
burden
lives   Yellow rain as abduction
            of a wound
                                    For the matter
                                    of shock

                          Magnified
                                    Toward a new coffer of
                                    bombs

            Someone dies for
              another to live
                                          How bent
                                          and never erstwhile
                                          this becomes
                                          my being

                          *

If to sculpt from fog
a child
of swords

Pronounce
question marks
on a beloved's face

My flooded cup

If it wails and grows thin
Trails the tenor of wind

*

For as long as a saola can
Flee, I have been brooding
             In my sleep moving through
A century of leaves. A voice
             Out of scrying, a river shifting
My ears. Some early mornings
             Are left for listening to water
Tones lilting the banks of a
             Primeval lake but the lake has
Been lacquered into the stars
             Mirroring its clotted hand
Down to mine. What does
             It take to raise an answer from
The grave, quantify stillness
             Of doubt through unmarked
Bodies becoming ciphers for
             Loss. I gather sharpness of my
Burn, beyond agony for an
             Answer: it is not to know
The shape of what happened
             But to know it happened, it
Happened, it happened. Here I
             Make my light to gaze the
Trail. Then sing this rain threadbare
             Into storm. If love is
The sacrament of digging, then
             Here I hold my found into fire.

And Yet Still More

That refugees somewhere and everywhere are waiting
That the waiting suffocates the ankles
That the body cannot be fed from the waiting
That the spew of shrapnel from hubris tongues enact the waiting
That waiting is never certain of itself
That waiting could change its mind overmorning
That waiting won't change its mind
That elbows cradle the waiting at night
That all are conceived and born into waiting
That the waiting can span the range of two continents
That waiting is a kind of forgetting and forgetting is the sea
That waiting is a silent syllable in never mind
That even the dead wait
That waiting is not the same as faith
That not all waiting is created equal
That waiting drips from the sap-hammer of a noose
That waiting turns-to-hunger-turns-to-water-turns-to-going-turns-to-too-late
That a refugee somewhere is waiting
That a refugee everywhere is waiting
That waiting has no documentation of its history
That refugees carry a surplus of waiting in plastic bags
That the ancestors wait
That waiting is given to refugees as a disease is given to the blood
That refugees wait
That all waiting floats into the exosphere
That refugee fathers sit outside of high schools waiting for the bell
That landmines excel at waiting
That a sleeping refugee is still waiting even in a state of dreaming
That most waiting happens in daylight
That wait and home are not spelled the same
That the refugee industry is built on the business of waiting
That refugees are put somewhere to wait
That refugees are put everywhere to wait
That wait is the refugee
That a refugee is waiting

That waiting must go on
That there is yet more waiting
That wait still and still more
That yet even
That next year
That the year after
That ever always
That more
That now
That wait is the refugee

Notes

What follows is a record of the documents and sources I used to craft the poems and works in this collection. In some cases, original text was excerpted from the document and integrated into my piece. In other instances, my piece draws from the information in the source document. Graphics and other visual elements were also extracted from the original documents.

The following sources were consulted in writing the series of untitled prose pieces:

Ahmad Alshannaq and Jae-Hyuk Yu's 2017 article "Occurrence, Toxicity, and Analysis of Major Mycotoxins in Food" published in Volume 14, Issue 6 of the *International Journal of Environmental Research and Public Health*.

Arms Control Association website for information on "The Biological Weapons Convention (BWC) at a Glance": https://www.armscontrol.org/factsheets/bwc.

Centers for Disease Control and Prevention website for information on "Case Definition: Trichothecene Mycotoxin" https://emergency.cdc.gov/agent/trichothecene/casedef.asp.

Department of State, United States, report to the Congress from Secretary of State Alexander M. Haig, Jr., published March 1982, Special Report No. 98 "Chemical Warfare in Southeast Asia and Afghanistan."

Department of State, United States, report to the Congress from Secretary of State George P. Shultz, published November 1982, Special Report No. 104 "Chemical Warfare in Southeast Asia and Afghanistan: An Update."

Grant Evans's 1983 book *The Yellow Rainmakers: Are Chemical Weapons Being Used in Southeast Asia?*, published by Verso Editions.

Jane Hamilton-Merritt's 1993 book *Tragic Mountains: The Hmong, the Americans, and the Secret Wars for Laos, 1942–1992*, published by Indiana University Press.

Rebecca Katz's 2005 PhD dissertation *Yellow Rain Revisited: Lessons Learned for the Investigation of Chemical and Biological Weapons Allegations*, completed at Princeton University, UMI Number: 3161973.

Matthew S. Meselson and Julian Perry Robinson's 2008 essay "The Yellow Rain Affair: Lessons from a Discredited Allegation" in *Terrorism, War, Or Disease? Unraveling the Use of Biological Weapons*, published by Stanford University Press and edited by Anne L. Clunan, Peter R. Lavoy, and Susan B. Martin.

Sterling Seagrave's 1981 book *Yellow Rain: A Journey through the Terror of Chemical Warfare*, published by M. Evans and Company, Inc.

Jonathan B. Tucker's 2001 article "The 'Yellow Rain' Controversy: Lessons for Arms Control Compliance," published in the Spring 2001 issue of the *Nonproliferation Review*.

Thomas Whiteside's articles "Annals of the Cold War: The Yellow-Rain Complex—I" and "Annals of the Cold War: The Yellow-Rain Complex—II," published in the *New Yorker* February 11, 1991, and February 18, 1991, respectively.

"The Fact of the Matter Is the Consequence of Ugly Deaths"

This poem's epigraph was excerpted from:

Radiolab episode "Yellow Rain" airing on September 23, 2012, WYNC Studios, hosted by Jad Abumrad and Robert Krulwich, produced by Pat Walters. The episode can be accessed online here: https://www.wnycstudios.org/story/239549-yellow-rain.

The watermark graphic was pulled from:

A declassified cable, date unknown, routing unknown, subject heading unknown, in Chemical Biological Weapons (CBW) Box 1 (Cables, Southeast Asia), National Security Archive.

"Anthem for Taking Back"

The declassified photograph of the Hmong men standing together was pulled from:

A folder of photographs, date unknown, subject heading unknown. Declassified by the Defense Intelligence Agency (DIA) April 24, 2003, declassification #153257, Armed Forces Medical Intelligence Center.

"A Body Always Yours"

This poem's epigraphs were excerpted from:

A declassified cable, dated November 20, 1979, routing unknown, subject heading unknown, in CBW Box 5 (Cables 1978–1987), National Security Archive.

A declassified report questionnaire attachment, dated February 13, 1980, in CBW Box 5 (Reports, Articles, Papers, and Memoranda 1979–1981), National Security Archive.

"Ill of the Dubious"

The information for this poem was drawn from:

A declassified Foreign Intelligence Information Report by the CIA, subject heading: "1. Poisoning of Hmong Refugees with Contaminated Pork, 2. Secondhand Account of Poison Gas Attacks," dated February 19, 1980, in CBW Box 5 (Reports, Articles, Papers, and Memoranda 1979–1981), National Security Archive.

"When the Poison Fell, Before 1979"

The italicized areas in this poem were excerpted from:

A declassified report by Herbert E. Segal, M.D., printed on the letterhead of the United States Army Medical Component, Armed Forces Research Institute of Medical Sciences, subject heading: "Trip Report, Chemical agent use, Hmong refugee populations," dated January 2, 1980, in CBW Box 5 (Reports, Articles, Papers, and Memoranda 1979–1981), National Security Archive.

"A Daub of Tree Swallows as Aerial Ash"

This poem's epigraph was excerpted from:
> A declassified cable, dated September 3, 1985, from the US Embassy in Bangkok to the Secretary of State in Washington, DC, subject heading: "Alleged atrocity in Laos," in CBW Box 1 (Cables, Southeast Asia), National Security Archive.

"Case Studies in Escape, Post-1975"

The information and some of the text for this poem were drawn and excerpted from:
> A media report by Hong Kong AFP (Agence France-Presse) "Refugees in Thailand say Laos using gas warfare," dated December 21, 1977, as published in the Foreign Broadcast Information Service, FBIS-APA-77-247, Daily Report, Asia and Pacific, distributed on December 23, 1977, page I3.

> A media report by Joel Henry for Hong Kong AFP "Poison gas being used against Meo rebels," dated September 27, 1978, as published in the FBIS, Volume IV, No. 188, distributed on October 13, 1978. Declassified by DIA July 18, 2003, declassification #159219, Armed Forces Medical Intelligence Center.

> A declassified cable, dated September 2, 1980, from the US Embassy in Bangkok to the Secretary of State in Washington, DC, subject heading: "Hmong refugees escape description," in CBW Box 5 (Cables 1978–1987), National Security Archive.

> A declassified cable, dated October 16, 1981, routing unknown, subject heading: "'Yellow rain' and more pressure against Hmong in Laos reported," in CBW Box 5 (Cables 1978–1987), National Security Archive.

The watermark map graphic was pulled from:
> A United States Department of State report to the Congress from Secretary of State Alexander M. Haig, Jr., "Chemical Warfare in Southeast Asia and Afghanistan," Special Report No. 98, dated March 22, 1982.

"Fewer Hmong Are Dying Now Than in the Past"

The title and italicized areas in this poem were excerpted from:
> A report, dated March 27, 1982, subject heading: "Nong Khai trip 24–26 March 1982, blood specimens." Declassified by DIA April 24, 2003, declassification #153359, Armed Forces Medical Intelligence Center.

> A Special National Intelligence Estimate report by the CIA, SNIE 11/50/37–82, "Use of Toxins and Other Lethal Chemicals in Southeast Asia and Afghanistan," dated March 2, 1983. Declassified May 5, 2008, document number: CIA-RDP86T00302R000701160015-4. CREST, General CIA records. Published on Central Intelligence Agency FOIA (http://www.foia.cia.gov).

A declassified cable, dated July 16, 1983, from the US Embassy in Bangkok to the Secretary of State in Washington, DC, subject heading: "Alleged continuing CBW use in Laos," in CBW Box 1 (Cables, Southeast Asia), National Security Archive.

"Signal for the Way Out"

The information for this poem was drawn from:

The responses of a Hmong refugee in a CBW Illness Survey Report questionnaire, dated March 7, 1984. Declassified by DIA November 17, 2003, declassification #153116, Armed Forces Medical Intelligence Center.

The graphic of the specimen containers was pulled from:

A report on the autopsy results of a yellow rain victim, testing conducted in May 1982. Declassified by DIA October 9, 2003, declassification #152531, Armed Forces Medical Intelligence Center.

"Self-Portrait Together as CBW Questionnaire"

The questionnaire structure of this poem was drawn from:

Questionnaires containing responses of Hmong refugees. Declassified by DIA November 17, 2003, declassification #153108, Armed Forces Medical Intelligence Center.

"Composition 1"

The information, text, and graphics for this work were drawn and excerpted from:

A memorandum, dated March 29, 1972, from Chief of Far East Division to Executive Director-Comptroller (W.E. Colby), subject heading: "Intelligence memorandum No. 0844/72 'The Meo of Northeast Laos: The Waning of a Tribe.'" Declassified October 28, 2004, document number: CIA-RDP80R01720R000700060059-1. CREST, General CIA records. Published on Central Intelligence Agency FOIA (http://www.foia.cia.gov).

A memorandum, dated March 31, 1972, from W.E. Colby to George Carver, Special Assistant for Vietnamese Affairs, subject heading: "Meo." Declassified October 28, 2004, document number: CIA-RDP80R01720R000700060059-1. CREST, General CIA records. Published on Central Intelligence Agency FOIA (http://www.foia.cia.gov).

A memorandum, dated May 20, 1975, from Donald F. Chamberlain, Inspector General, to the Director of Central Intelligence, subject heading: "CIA Activities at Fort Detrick, Frederick, Maryland." Declassified March 9, 2010, document number: 0005444835. CREST, FOIA Collection. Published on Central Intelligence Agency FOIA (http://www.foia.cia.gov).

A statement issued by W.E. Colby, Director of Central Intelligence, before the United States Senate Select Committee to Study Governmental Operations with Respect to Intelligence Activities, dated September 16, 1975. Declassified November 22, 2006, document number:

CIA-RDP82B00871R000100070006-9. CREST, General CIA records. Published on Central Intelligence Agency FOIA (http://www.foia.cia.gov).

A report to the Congress, by the Comptroller General of the United States, "Stockpile of Lethal Chemical Munitions and Agents—Better Management Needed, Department of Defense," dated September 14, 1977. Declassified January 1992, in CBW Box 13 (Chemical Biological Warfare FOIA), National Security Archive.

A declassified tracking and data compilation of yellow rain attacks, dated summer 1980 (estimate date, author unknown, title page missing), in CBW Box 5 (Reports, Articles, Papers, and Memoranda 1982–84, 1986–87, and 1989), National Security Archive.

An executive summary report by the Defense Science Board, Chemical Warfare Summer Study, Internal DoD Working Document, dated October 1980. Declassified March 4, 2014, document number: CIA-RDP93B01137R000400010062-5. CREST, General CIA records. Published on Central Intelligence Agency FOIA (http://www.foia.cia.gov).

A declassified handwritten ledger "Yellow Gas" charting the names of victims and their symptoms, dated November 25, 1981, in CBW Box 5 (Reports, Articles, Papers, and Memoranda 1979–1981), National Security Archive.

Articles published in *Covert Action Information Bulletin*, Number 17 (Summer 1982), "Agent Exposes Secret Mission" and "Excerpts from CAIB—Scott Barnes Interview." Declassified June 9, 2010, document number: CIA-RDP90-00845R000100180005-3. CREST, General CIA records. Published on Central Intelligence Agency FOIA (http://www.foia.cia.gov).

An article, dated July 17, 1988, in the *Deseret News* by Lee Davidson, "Agencies deny man's charges of POWs, chemical arms, murder in Southeast Asia."

"Blood Cooperation"

This poem's epigraphs were excerpted from:
A declassified cable, dated October 28, 1983, from the US Embassy in Bangkok to the Secretary of State in Washington, DC, subject heading: "Hmong CBW sample," in CBW Box 1 (Cables, Southeast Asia and Afghanistan), National Security Archive.

A cable, dated April 19, 1984, from the US Embassy in Bangkok to multiple agencies, subject heading: "CBW biological control samples." Declassified by DIA November 17, 2003, declassification #153125, Armed Forces Medical Intelligence Center.

The following source was also consulted:
A cable, dated May 9, 1984, from the US Embassy in Bangkok to multiple agencies, subject heading: "Hmong leadership pressure for CBW test results." Declassified by DIA October 15, 2003, declassification #152621, Armed Forces Medical Intelligence Center.

The watermark graphic was pulled from:

A report containing photographs of test vials and labels, date unknown. Declassified by DIA October 9, 2003, declassification #152518, Armed Forces Medical Intelligence Center.

"Specimens from Ban Vinai Camp, 1983"

The italicized areas in this poem were excerpted from:

A report of specimen samples, dated February 16, 1983. Declassified by DIA April 24, 2003, declassification #153264, Armed Forces Medical Intelligence Center.

The watermark graphic was pulled from:

A memorandum on routing of samples, dated August 20, 1980 (estimate). Declassified by DIA October 15, 2003, declassification #152539, Armed Forces Medical Intelligence Center.

"Authorization to Depart Ravaged Homeland as Biomedical Sample"

The information for this poem was drawn from:

A report, date unknown with earliest date in document shown as May 29, 1982, page heading: "Foreign Material Exploitation Interim Report, Analysis of Tissue Samples From a Victim of an Alleged Yellow Rain Attack." Declassified by DIA October 9, 2003, declassification #152531, Armed Forces Medical Intelligence Center.

"Arriving as Lost"

This poem's epigraph was excerpted from:

A cable, dated August 20, 1980, from the US Defense Attaché Office in Bangkok to the US Army Medical Intelligence and Information Agency, subject heading: "Blood samples from alleged Hmong gassing victims." Declassified by DIA October 15, 2003, declassification #152539, Armed Forces Medical Intelligence Center.

The following sources were also consulted:

A memorandum for record, dated November 23, 1981, routing unknown, subject heading: "Courier activities on 20 November 1981." Declassified by DIA April 18, 2003, declassification #152509, Armed Forces Medical Intelligence Center.

A cable, dated March 10, 1982, routing unknown, subject heading: "Tech escort support." Declassified by DIA October 9, 2003, declassification #152511, Armed Forces Medical Intelligence Center.

A cover letter, dated April 22, 1982, from the US Embassy in Bangkok addressed "To Whom It May Concern," regarding blood samples contained herein. Declassified by DIA November 14, 2003, declassification #153361, Armed Forces Medical Intelligence Center.

A memorandum, dated February 8, 1983, from US Government, LTC, AARMA (name redacted) to unknown person, subject heading: "Transportation of CBW samples." Declassified by DIA April 24, 2003, declassification #153278, Armed Forces Medical Intelligence Center.

The watermark graphic was pulled from:

An assemblage of forms and paperwork, date unknown. Declassified by DIA April 18, 2003, declassification #152524, Armed Forces Medical Intelligence Center.

"Ever Tenuous"

The fragments of text in this work were excerpted from:

A cable, dated July 24, 1980, routing unknown, page heading: "Pentagon Telecommunications Center," subject heading: "Samples from alleged gassing victims." Declassified by DIA October 15, 2003, declassification #152535, Armed Forces Medical Intelligence Center.

A cable, dated December 12, 1980, from the Director of US AMIAA Fort Detrick, Maryland to the US Defense Attaché Office in Bangkok, subject heading: "Computerized medical questionnaire." Declassified by DIA April 24, 2003, declassification #153050, Armed Forces Medical Intelligence Center.

A report of sample analyses results, dated January 3, 1983, page heading: "Results of analyses." Declassified by DIA April 22, 2003, declassification #152515, Armed Forces Medical Intelligence Center.

A cable confirming receipt of samples, dated February 1, 1983, from the Director of AFMIC Fort Detrick, Maryland to HQDA Washington, DC and FSTC Intel Ops Charlottesville, Virginia, subject heading: "Spot report – receipt of CW/BW biomedical samples." Declassified by DIA April 23, 2003, declassification #152598, Armed Forces Medical Intelligence Center.

A cable, dated February 22, 1984, from FSTC Intel Ops in Charlottesville, Virginia to the US Embassy in Bangkok, subject heading: "CBW samples." Declassified by DIA October 9, 2003, declassification #152519, Armed Forces Medical Intelligence Center.

A report, dated May 9, 1984, page heading: "Category III statistics." Declassified by DIA April 23, 2003, declassification #152902, Armed Forces Medical Intelligence Center.

A report of sample analyses results, dated October 10, 1984. Declassified by DIA April 23, 2003, declassification #152536, Armed Forces Medical Intelligence Center.

A cable, dated October 25, 1984, from the Director of AFMIC Fort Detrick, Maryland to FSTC Intel Ops Charlottesville, Virginia, subject heading: "CBT sample exploitation project – weekly report." Declassified by DIA April 23, 2003, declassification #152596, Armed Forces Medical Intelligence Center.

A cable, dated October 31, 1984, routing unknown, subject heading: "Breakage problems." Declassified by DIA October 21, 2003, declassification #152642, Armed Forces Medical Intelligence Center.

A cable, dated February 7, 1985, from the Director of AFMIC Fort Detrick, Maryland to the US Embassy in Bangkok, subject heading: "CBW samples." Declassified by DIA October 21, 2003, declassification #152642, Armed Forces Medical Intelligence Center.

"Futile to Find You"

This poem's epigraphs were excerpted from:

A memorandum, dated October 23, 1979, from Chief of Clinical Resources Group (name redacted) to Commander of US Army Biomedical Laboratory, subject heading: "Trip report." Declassified by DIA April 23, 2003, declassification #152540, Armed Forces Medical Intelligence Center.

A cable, dated July 10, 1980, from Commander FSTC Charlottesville, Virginia to the US Defense Attaché Office in Bangkok, subject heading: "Medical samples from alleged gassing victim." Declassified by DIA April 23, 2003, declassification #152538, Armed Forces Medical Intelligence Center.

A cable, dated January 29, 1981, from the US Defense Attaché Office in Bangkok to the Defense Intelligence Agency in Washington, DC, subject heading: "Chemical warfare." Declassified by DIA April 23, 2003, declassification #152540, Armed Forces Medical Intelligence Center.

A memorandum, dated June 4, 1982, from unknown (name redacted) to Commander US AMRDC, page heading: "Disposition form," subject heading: "Toxicity testing of overseas water sample." Declassified by DIA April 23, 2003, declassification #152901, Armed Forces Medical Intelligence Center.

A cable, dated March 14, 1983, from the Director of AFMIC Fort Detrick, Maryland to FSTC Intel Ops in Charlottesville, Virginia, subject heading: "Spot report no. 2." Declassified by DIA April 23, 2003, declassification #152598, Armed Forces Medical Intelligence Center.

A memorandum, dated April 23, 1984, from Intelligence Research Analyst (name redacted) to the Director of AFMIC, subject heading: "Sample analysis summaries." Declassified by DIA August 8, 2003, declassification #152651, Armed Forces Medical Intelligence Center.

The graphic was pulled from:

A report cover page, date unknown, routing unknown, subject heading: "Instructions regarding handling/routing of contents." Declassified by DIA October 9, 2003, declassification #152533, Armed Forces Medical Intelligence Center.

"Procedures in Hunt of Wreckage"

The italicized areas in this poem were excerpted from:

A report of sample analyses results, dated August 3, 1982. Declassified by DIA October 15, 2003, declassification #152529, Armed Forces Medical Intelligence Center.

A report of sample analyses results, dated October 12, 1982. Declassified by DIA October 9, 2003, declassification #152533, Armed Forces Medical Intelligence Center.

The graphic was pulled from:

A report of sample analyses results, gas chromatography-mass spectrometry (GC/MS) chart, dated November 3, 1981. Declassified by DIA October 9, 2003, declassification #152533, Armed Forces Medical Intelligence Center.

"Disfigures"

This poem's epigraphs were excerpted from:

A cable, dated March 2, 1984, routing unknown, subject heading: "CBW investigative team funding." Declassified by DIA October 21, 2003, declassification #152642, Armed Forces Medical Intelligence Center.

A memorandum for the record, dated May 9, 1984, subject heading: "CW/BW Sample Exploitation Project." Declassified by DIA April 23, 2003, declassification #152902, Armed Forces Medical Intelligence Center.

"Request for Furthermore"

The italicized areas in this poem were excerpted from:

A cable, dated February 28, 1984, from the Director of AFMIC Fort Detrick, Maryland to the US Embassy in Bangkok, Secretary of State in Washington, DC, Secretary of Defense in Washington, DC, subject heading: "Re-interview of alleged CW victims." Declassified by DIA October 21, 2003, declassification #152642, Armed Forces Medical Intelligence Center.

A cable, dated April 18, 1984, from the Director of AFMIC Fort Detrick, Maryland to the US Embassy in Bangkok, subject heading: "CBW biologic control program." Declassified by DIA October 21, 2003, declassification #152642, Armed Forces Medical Intelligence Center.

A cable, dated January 29, 1985, from the Director of AFMIC Fort Detrick, Maryland to the US Embassy in Bangkok, subject heading: "Follow-up sampling." Declassified by DIA October 21, 2003, declassification #152642, Armed Forces Medical Intelligence Center.

"We Can't Confirm Yellow Rain Happened, We Can't Confirm It Didn't"

This poem's epigraphs were excerpted from:

A paper, dated March 1980, "Chemical and Biological Warfare: Analysis of Recent Reports Concerning the Soviet Union and Vietnam," by J.P. Perry Robinson, Science Policy Research Unit, University of Sussex, in Center for National Security Studies Box 1 (CBW Articles and Documents 1960–1980), National Security Archive.

A memorandum, dated August 29, 1980, from the Assistant Surgeon General for Research and Development (name redacted) to the Office of the Under Secretary of Defense for Research and Engineering (name redacted), subject heading: "Mideast investigation of chemical agent exposure." Declassified by DIA April 23, 2003, declassification #152541, Armed Forces Medical Intelligence Center.

A memorandum report, dated November 18, 1980, from the Department of the Army, US Army Medical Intelligence and Information Agency in Fort Detrick, Maryland (name redacted) to multiple agencies, subject heading: "Evaluation of biological samples – final report." Declassified by DIA April 23, 2003, declassification #152541, Armed Forces Medical Intelligence Center.

A declassified cable, dated December 1, 1982, from the US Mission of the United Nations in New York to the Secretary of State in Washington, DC, subject heading: "Report on UN chemical weapons (CW) experts," in CBW Box 1 (Cables, Southeast Asia and Afghanistan), National Security Archive.

A Special National Intelligence Estimate report by the CIA, SNIE 11/50/37–82, "Use of Toxins and Other Lethal Chemicals in Southeast Asia and Afghanistan," dated March 2, 1983. Declassified May 5, 2008, document number: CIA-RDP86T00302R000701160015-4. CREST, General CIA records. Published on Central Intelligence Agency FOIA (http://www.foia.cia.gov).

A memorandum, dated July 5, 1985, from Sharon A. Watson, PhD, Research Toxicologist to unknown (name redacted), subject heading: "Compilation of CW use data," reference heading: "Memorandum for MAJ John Weske, 25 Jun 85." Declassified April 1, 2010, document number: CIA-RDP87R00029R000400750017-6. CREST, General CIA records. Published on Central Intelligence Agency FOIA (http://www.foia.cia.gov).

A declassified cable, dated April 3, 1986, from the US Embassy in Bangkok to the Secretary of State in Washington, DC, subject heading: "Canadian study on yellow rain," in CBW Box 1 (Cables, Southeast Asia), National Security Archive.

A memorandum, dated May 14, 1986, from the Armed Forces Medical Intelligence Center in Fort Detrick, Maryland, to the Chairman of the CBW Use Committee, subject heading: "Current status of biomedical sampling program." Declassified by DIA August 8, 2003, declassification #159243, Armed Forces Medical Intelligence Center.

"Composition 2"

The information, text, and graphics for this work were drawn and excerpted from:

An article, dated August 8, 1974, "War research at British universities," published by *New Scientist*, Volume 63, No. 909, section title "Ethnic weapons?".

A Senate committee report, dated April 26, 1976, "Foreign and Military Intelligence, Book I, Final Report of the Select Committee to Study Governmental Operations with respect to Intelligence Activities, United States Senate." Report no. 94–755.

A report to the Congress, by the Comptroller General of the United States, "US Lethal Chemical Munitions Policy: Issues Facing the Congress," dated September 21, 1977. Declassified January 1992, in CBW Box 13 (Chemical Biological Warfare FOIA), National Security Archive.

A declassified media brief, "PRC, Kampuchean charges of SRV gas warfare," dated September 12, 1979, as published in the Foreign Broadcast Information Service trends, in CBW Box 5 (Reports, Articles, Papers, and Memoranda 1979–1981), National Security Archive.

A declassified tracking and data compilation of yellow rain attacks, dated summer 1980 (estimate date, author unknown, title page missing), in CBW Box 5 (Reports, Articles, Papers, and Memoranda 1982–84, 1986–87, and 1989), National Security Archive.

A declassified report, dated August 3, 1981, from Joseph J. Vervier, Acting Chief, Research Division, ATTN: DRDAR-RAI-C/Mr. Pfister, subject heading: "Analysis/evaluation of water and foliage samples," in CBW Box 5 (Reports, Articles, Papers, and Memoranda 1979–1981), National Security Archive.

A declassified cable, dated August 31, 1981, routing unknown, subject heading unknown, in CBW Box 5 (Cables 1978–1987), National Security Archive.

A declassified cable, dated January 15, 1982, from the US Embassy in Bangkok to the Secretary of State in Washington, DC, subject heading: "Proposals for CBW-related studies," in CBW Box 1 (Cables, Southeast Asia), National Security Archive.

A memorandum, dated April 25, 1983, from Chairman of Human Subjects Research Panel (name redacted) to Executive Director, subject heading: "Protection of human subjects of chemical/toxin weapons screening project." Declassified August 8, 2008, document number: CIA-RDP85B01152R000200220003-1. CREST, General CIA records. Published on Central Intelligence Agency FOIA (http://www.foia.cia.gov).

A memorandum for the record, dated June 14, 1983, subject heading: "Human subjects review panel procedures." Declassified August 8, 2008, document number: CIA-RDP85B01152R000200220002-2. CREST, General CIA records. Published on Central Intelligence Agency FOIA (http://www.foia.cia.gov).

A Special National Intelligence Estimate report by the CIA, SNIE 11-17-83, "Implications of Soviet Use of Chemical and Toxin Weapons for US Security Interests," dated September 15, 1983. Declassified May 27, 2009, document number: CIA-RDP86T00302R000601010002-5. CREST, General CIA records. Published on Central Intelligence Agency FOIA (http://www .foia.cia.gov).

A letter report, dated June 18, 1984, "Yellow Rain – Separating Fact from Fiction" by the Armed Forces Medical Intelligence Center. Declassified by DIA August 8, 2003, declassification #152651, Armed Forces Medical Intelligence Center.

Rebecca Katz's 2005 PhD dissertation, *Yellow Rain Revisited: Lessons Learned for the Investigation of Chemical and Biological Weapons Allegations*, completed at Princeton University, UMI Number: 3161973.

"This Demands the Vengeance of a Wolf"

This poem's epigraph was excerpted from:
A report of test results, dated March 25, 1981, Department of the Army, US Army Armament Research and Development Command, Chemical Systems Laboratory, Aberdeen Proving Ground, subject heading: "Sample 10027-D." Declassified by DIA August 12, 2003, declassification #159266, Armed Forces Medical Intelligence Center.

The graphic was pulled from:

A US Army field manual, dated November 9, 1979, FM 21-40, in Center for National Security Studies Box 1 (CBW Articles and Documents 1960–1980), National Security Archive.

"Agent Orange Commando Lava"

The italicized areas in this poem were excerpted from:

A declassified memorandum, dated January 13, 1967, from the Deputy Under Secretary of State for Political Affairs to the Secretary of State, subject heading: "Weather modification in North Vietnam and Laos (Project Popeye)." Department of State, Central Files, POL 27 VIET S. Top Secret. Drafted by Hamilton. *Foreign Relations of the United States*, 1964–1968, Volume XXVIII, Laos. Office of the Historian, US Department of State.

A declassified telegram, dated May 29, 1967, from the US Embassy in Laos to the Secretary of State in Washington, DC, subject heading: "Operation Commando Lava." Department of State, Central Files, POL 27 LAOS. Top Secret; Priority; Limdis. Repeated to Bangkok, Saigon, CINCPAC, COMUSMACV, CINCPACAF, and JCS. *Foreign Relations of the United States*, 1964–1968, Volume XXVIII, Laos. Office of the Historian, US Department of State.

A memorandum, dated June 1, 1967, from George A. Carver, Jr., Special Assistant for Vietnamese Affairs, to Mr. William C. Hamilton, Laos Country Director, Bureau of East Asian and Pacific Affairs, Department of State, subject heading: "Soil destabilization project." Declassified August 19, 2004, document number: CIA-RDP80R01720R000500070154-6. CREST, General CIA records. Published on Central Intelligence Agency FOIA (http://www .foia.cia.gov).

A declassified cable, dated July 9, 1982, from the US Mission of the United Nations in New York to the Secretary of State in Washington, DC, subject heading: "Vietnamese report on US chemical warfare," in CBW Box 1 (Cables, Southeast Asia), National Security Archive.

"Toxicology Conference Proposal"

The italicized areas in this poem were excerpted from:

A conference abstract proposal form, submitted to the Society of Toxicology, 1986 Annual Meeting, by the Pathophysiology Division, US Army Medical Research Institute of Infectious Diseases, Fort Detrick, Maryland. Declassified by DIA August 12, 2003, declassification #159273, Armed Forces Medical Intelligence Center.

"Smear of Petals"

This poem's epigraphs were excerpted from:

A memorandum for the record, dated April 29, 1971, from John M. Maury, Legislative Counsel, subject heading: "Conversation with Senator George McGovern re: drug problem in Southeast Asia." Declassified August 30, 2001, document number: CIA-RDP73B00296R000300060019-3.

CREST, General CIA records. Published on Central Intelligence Agency FOIA (http://www .foia.cia.gov).

A cable, dated July 19, 1973, from the Secretary of State in Washington, DC, to the US Embassy in Vientiane, subject heading: "Reported use of herbicides/defoliants in narcotics suppression program." Declassified June 30, 2005, US Department of State.

The watermark graphic was pulled from:
A declassified cable, dated November 20, 1979, routing unknown, subject heading unknown, in CBW Box 5 (Cables 1978–1987), National Security Archive.

"Syndrome Sleep Death Sudden"

The italicized areas in this poem were excerpted from:
A memorandum, dated December 18, 1981, from the Director of Scientific and Weapons Research (name redacted) to the Director and Deputy Director of Central Intelligence, subject heading: "Recent developments on 'yellow rain.'" Declassified by DIA May 20, 2003, declassification #155283, Armed Forces Medical Intelligence Center.

A report, dated December 1, 1982, by Richard C. Harruff, MD, PhD, "Chemical Warfare in Southeast Asia – Personal Observations." Declassified February 1, 2010, document number: CIA-RDP87R00029R000400800002-6. CREST, General CIA records. Published on Central Intelligence Agency FOIA (http://www.foia.cia.gov).

An article by Ronald G. Munger, PhD, "Sudden Death in Sleep of Laotian-Hmong Refugees in Thailand: A Case-Control Study," published in the *American Journal of Public Health*, September 1987, Volume 77, Number 9.

The watermark graphic was pulled from:
A declassified cable, dated April 1, 1985, from the US Embassy in Bangkok to the Secretary of State in Washington, DC, subject heading: "Fifth quarterly report of CBW field team chief," in CBW Box 1 (Cables, Southeast Asia), National Security Archive.

"Skin as a Vehicle for Experimentation"

The italicized and redacted areas in this poem were excerpted from:
A declassified report, dated December 24, 1971, "(redacted) As a Vehicle for Experimentation," author unknown, prepared by (redacted) as part of a government contract, in Center for National Security Studies Box 1 (CBW Articles and Documents 1960–1980), National Security Archive.

"A Moment Still Waiting for You"

This poem's epigraphs were excerpted from:
A declassified report, dated December 31, 1981, "Trichothecenes and the Possibility That They Could Be Chemical Warfare Samples," Armed Forces Medical Intelligence Center, in CBW Box 5 (Reports, Articles, Papers, and Memoranda 1979–1981), National Security Archive.

A declassified letter report, dated December 15, 1981, from Philip S. Thayer, PhD, Consultant at Arthur D. Little Inc., to Mr. Steve Singer, American Broadcasting Company, attention: "Rain of Terror" *ABC News Closeup*, Steve Singer, Producer; in CBW Box 5 (Reports, Articles, Papers, and Memoranda 1982–84, 1986–87, and 1989), National Security Archive.

A declassified cable, dated June 15, 1982, from the US Mission US NATO to the Secretary of State in Washington, DC, subject heading: "Canadian report on CW use in Southeast Asia," in CBW Box 1 (Cables, Southeast Asia), National Security Archive.

A letter report, dated June 18, 1984, "Yellow Rain – Separating Fact from Fiction" by the Armed Forces Medical Intelligence Center. Declassified by DIA August 8, 2003, declassification #152651, Armed Forces Medical Intelligence Center.

The watermark graphic was pulled from:
The image of a folder, date unknown, author unknown. Declassified by DIA April 23, 2003, declassification #152532, Armed Forces Medical Intelligence Center.

"Composition 3"

The information and most of the text for this work were drawn and excerpted from:
A report, date unknown with latest date in document shown as November 29, 1983, from Dr. H. Cohen forwarding comments on External Affairs Canada, (redacted) Geneva, and (redacted) USA (who sent documentation referred to in the (redacted) Report (Geneva) and others), subject heading: "Dr. H. Cohen on 'Yellow Rain' and others." Declassified by DIA August 12, 2003, declassification #159255, Armed Forces Medical Intelligence Center.

A declassified memorandum and attachment, dated July 2, 1984, from the United States Arms Control and Disarmament Agency to multiple agencies, subject heading: "Meselson point paper," in CBW Box 5 (Reports, Articles, Papers, and Memoranda 1982–84, 1986–87, and 1989), National Security Archive.

An article, dated January 24, 1985, "Yellow rain and the bee faeces theory," published in Volume 313 of *Nature*, by Joseph D. Rosen, Huguette Cohen, Chester J. Mirocha, and H. Bruno Schiefer.

An article, dated September 1985, "Yellow Rain," published in Volume 253, Number 3, of *Scientific American*, by Thomas D. Seeley, Joan W. Nowicke, Matthew Meselson, Jeanne Guillemin, and Pongthep Akratanakul.

An article, dated Autumn 1987, "Yellow Rain: The Story Collapses," published in Number 68 of *Foreign Policy*, by Julian Robinson, Jeanne Guillemin, and Matthew Meselson.

A 2008 article, "The Yellow Rain Affair: Lessons from a Discredited Allegation," by Matthew S. Meselson and Julian Perry Robinson, published by Stanford Security Studies, an imprint of Stanford University Press, in the book *Terrorism, War, or Disease? Unraveling the Use of Biological Weapons*, edited by Anne L. Clunan, Peter R. Lavoy, and Susan B. Martin.

"Sverdlovsk"

The information and epigraphs for this poem were drawn and excerpted from:

An article, dated 1997, "The Anthrax Solution: The Sverdlovsk Incident and the Resolution of a Biological Weapons Controversy," by Michael D. Gordin, published in Volume 30, Issue 3, of the *Journal of the History of Biology*.

An article, dated February 18, 1991, "Annals of the Cold War: The Yellow-Rain Complex—II," by Thomas Whiteside, published in the *New Yorker*.

The following sources were also consulted:

A Congressional committee hearing report, dated April 24, 1980, "Strategic Implications of Chemical and Biological Warfare," Hearing Before the Subcommittees on International Security and Scientific Affairs and on Asian and Pacific Affairs of the Committee on Foreign Affairs, Ninety-Sixth Congress, Second Session.

An article, dated 1991, "A Return to Sverdlovsk: Allegations of Soviet Activities Related to Biological Weapons," by Milton Leitenberg, published in Volume 12, Issue 2, of *Arms Control*.

"Never to Have Had Your Song Blessed"

This poem's epigraph was excerpted from:

A declassified memorandum and attachment, dated July 2, 1984, from the United States Arms Control and Disarmament Agency to multiple agencies, subject heading: "Meselson point paper," authored by C. Stettner, in CBW Box 5 (Reports, Articles, Papers, and Memoranda 1982–84, 1986–87, and 1989), National Security Archive.

"Notes in Rebuttal: What They May Have Known about the Possibility"

The italicized areas in this poem were excerpted from:

A Congressional committee hearing report, dated April 30, 1969, "Chemical and Biological Warfare," Hearing before the Committee on Foreign Relations, United States Senate, Ninety-First Congress, First Session. Secret hearing held on April 30, 1969; sanitized and printed on June 23, 1969.

"All of a Sudden, Yellow Spots"

This poem's epigraph was excerpted from:

An article, dated February 11, 1991, "Annals of the Cold War: The Yellow-Rain Complex—I," by Thomas Whiteside, published in the *New Yorker*.

"Recantation for the Quieting"

The information and epigraphs for this poem were drawn and excerpted from:

A declassified cable, dated January 5, 1984, routing unknown, subject heading: "Alleged use of CBW/yellow rain against Hmong," in CBW Box 5 (Cables 1978–1987), National Security Archive.

A Congressional committee hearing report, dated March 30 and July 13, 1982, "Foreign Policy and Arms Control Implications of Chemical Weapons," Hearings before the Subcommittees on International Security and Scientific Affairs and on Asian and Pacific Affairs of the Committee on Foreign Affairs, House of Representatives, Ninety-Seventh Congress, Second Session.

The following sources were also consulted:

An article, dated Autumn 1987, "Yellow Rain: The Story Collapses," published in Number 68 of *Foreign Policy*, by Julian Robinson, Jeanne Guillemin, and Matthew Meselson.

A 2008 article, "The Yellow Rain Affair: Lessons from a Discredited Allegation," by Matthew S. Meselson and Julian Perry Robinson, published by Stanford Security Studies, an imprint of Stanford University Press, in the book *Terrorism, War, or Disease? Unraveling the Use of Biological Weapons*, edited by Anne L. Clunan, Peter R. Lavoy, and Susan B. Martin.

"Il/Logic, Fully Unvetted: A Makeshift Analysis of the Behavior of Southeast Asian Honeybees"

The italicized areas in this poem were excerpted from:

A 2011 article, "Absconding, Migration and Swarming," by H. R. Hepburn, published by Springer in the book *Honeybees of Asia*, edited by Randall Hepburn and Sarah E. Radloff.

Rebecca Katz's 2005 PhD dissertation, *Yellow Rain Revisited: Lessons Learned for the Investigation of Chemical and Biological Weapons Allegations*, completed at Princeton University, UMI Number: 3161973.

An article, dated September 2012, "Migrating Giant Honey Bees (*Apis dorsata*) Congregate Annually at Stopover site in Thailand," by Willard S. Robinson published in Volume 7, Issue 9, of *PLOS ONE*.

An article, dated August 3, 2000, "Giant honeybees return to their nest sites," by J. Paar, B. P. Oldroyd, and G. Kastberger, published in Volume 406 of *Nature*.

A 2005 article, "Periodic mass flights of the giant honey bee *Apis dorsata* in successive days at two nesting sites in different environmental conditions," by Jerzy Wilde, Chandrashekhara C. Reddy, and Narayanappa Nagaraja, published in Volume 44, Issue 4, of *Journal of Apicultural Research*.

A 1996 article, "Behavioural features of a periodic form of massed flight activity in the giant honeybee *Apis dorsata*," by G. Kastberger, O. Winder, T. Hoetzl, and G. Raspotnig, published in Volume 27, Number 5, of *Apidologie*.

The following sources were also consulted:

An article, dated June 1994, "Colony migration in the tropical honey bee *Apis dorsata* F. (Hymenoptera: Apidae)," by Fred C. Dyer and Thomas D. Seeley, published in Volume 41, Issue 2, of *Insectes Sociaux*.

An article, dated August 3, 2000, "Home-site fidelity in migratory honeybees," by Peter Neumann, Nikolaus Koeniger, Gudrun Koeniger, Salim Tingek, Per Kryger, and Robin F. A. Moritz, published in Volume 406 of *Nature*.

"Allied with the Bees"

The information and epigraph for this poem were drawn and excerpted from:

A copy of a letter to the editor, dated April 6, 1984, by S. Yang in Long Beach, California, newspaper unknown, in CBW Box 5 (Reports, Articles, Papers, and Memoranda 1982–84, 1986–87, and 1989), National Security Archive.

A declassified cable, dated November 5, 1984, from the US Embassy in Bangkok to the Secretary of State in Washington, DC, subject heading: "CBW Samples," in CBW Box 1 (Cables, Southeast Asia), National Security Archive.

"Composition 4"

The information, text, and graphics for this work were drawn and excerpted from:

A declassified report, date unknown with latest date in document shown as February 25, 1952, subject heading: "Study by the Joint Advanced Study Committee on Biological Warfare," in Center for National Security Studies Box 1 (Documents on CBW, including their use against Vietnamese), National Security Archive.

A Congressional report, dated March 22, 1962, "Importation of Honey Bees," House of Representatives, 87th Congress, Second Session, Report no. 1477. Declassified April 13, 2005, document number: CIA-RDP64B00346R000300100002-0. CREST, General CIA records. Published on Central Intelligence Agency FOIA (http://www.foia.cia.gov).

A cable, dated July 15, 1974, from the Secretary of State in Washington, DC to the US Embassy in New Delhi, subject heading: "DHEW/PHS/FDA/SFCP – Project 01-617-4, Aflatoxin toxicity in non-human primates." Declassified June 30, 2005, US Department of State.

A memorandum and report attachment, dated April 8, 1976, from David H. Blee, Acting Deputy Director for Operations, Central Intelligence Agency, to the Director of Central Intelligence, subject heading and report title: "Military Thoughts (USSR), the Employment of Biological Weapons." Declassified date unknown, document number: 5076e965993247d4d82b67db. Special Collection, Soviet and Warsaw Pact Military Journals. Published on Central Intelligence Agency FOIA (http://www.foia.cia.gov).

A report, dated April 30, 1976, routing unknown, subject heading and report title: "Military Thoughts (USSR), Biological Weapons and Some Problems of Antibiological Defense." Declassified April 12, 2012, document number: CIA-RDP10-00105R000201850001-0. CREST, General CIA records. Published on Central Intelligence Agency FOIA (http://www.foia.cia.gov).

A memorandum for the record, dated July 13, 1982, subject heading: "Meeting with COL Robinson, HQDA DCSOPS on 9 July 82." Declassified October 23, 2007, document number: CIA-RDP85-00024R000400400018-4. CREST, General CIA records. Published on Central Intelligence Agency FOIA (http://www.foia.cia.gov).

A Special National Intelligence Estimate report by the CIA, SNIE 11/50/37-82JX, "Use of Toxins and Other Lethal Chemicals in Southeast Asia and Afghanistan, Volume I, Key Judgements," dated February 2, 1983. Declassified October 4, 1997, document number: 0000284013. FOIA, National Intelligence Council (NIC) Collection. Published on Central Intelligence Agency FOIA (http://www.foia.cia.gov).

A declassified Special National Intelligence Estimate report by the CIA, SNIE number unknown, "Implications of Soviet Use of Chemical and Toxin Weapons for US Security Interests," dated September 13, 1983, in CBW Box 5 (Reports, Articles, Papers, and Memoranda 1982–84, 1986–87, and 1989), National Security Archive.

An article, dated September 1985, "Yellow Rain," published in Volume 253, Number 3, of *Scientific American*, by Thomas D. Seeley, Joan W. Nowicke, Matthew Meselson, Jeanne Guillemin, and Pongthep Akratanakul.

A 1987 book, *BOHICA*, by Scott Barnes, published by BOHICA Corporation, Daring Books.

A declassified cable, date unknown, routing unknown, subject heading unknown, in CBW Box 1 (Cables, Southeast Asia), National Security Archive.

"Noxious"

The following source was consulted:
A Congressional committee hearing report, dated December 12, 1979, "Use of Chemical Agents in Southeast Asia since the Vietnam War," Hearing before the Subcommittee on Asian and Pacific Affairs of the Committee on Foreign Affairs, House of Representatives, Ninety-Sixth Congress, First Session.

"Orderly Wrap-Up of CBW Investigation"

This poem's epigraph was excerpted from:
A declassified cable, dated October 25, 1986, from the Secretary of State in Washington, DC to US Embassy in Bangkok, subject heading: "Orderly wrap up of CBW investigation," in CBW Box 1 (Cables, Southeast Asia), National Security Archive.

"Revolt of Bees"

This poem's epigraph was excerpted from:
A research paper, "Military Application of Apiculture: The (Other) Nature of War" by Lois Delaney, submitted in partial fulfillment for the degree of Master of Military Studies, US Marine Corps, Command and Staff College, Marine Corps University, March 30, 2011.

"Composition 5"

The information, text, and graphics for this work were drawn and excerpted from:

A declassified report to the Congress, by the Comptroller General of the United States, "US Lethal Chemical Munitions Policy: Issues Facing the Congress, Department of Defense," dated September 21, 1977, in CBW Box 13 (Chemical Biological Warfare FOIA), National Security Archive.

A memorandum report, dated September 23, 1981, from the Department of State, Director of Bureau of Politico-Military Affairs to multiple agencies, subject heading: "CBW Arms Control," report title "Strategy for CBW Arms Control." Declassified October 23, 2007, document number: CIA-RDP84B00049R000400820002-7. CREST, General CIA records. Published on Central Intelligence Agency FOIA (http://www.foia.cia.gov).

An editorial in the *New York Times* by Nicholas Wade, dated November 23, 1983, "The Editorial Notebook; The Embarrassment of 'Yellow Rain.'"

An article in the *Wall Street Journal* by William Kucewicz, dated May 30, 1984, "Mycotoxins: The Scientific Battlefield."

An article in the *Wall Street Journal* by William Kucewicz, dated September 6, 1985, "The 'Bee Feces' Theory Undone."

A declassified cable, dated November 15, 1985, from the US Embassy in Bangkok to the Secretary of State in Washington, DC, subject heading: "Seventh quarterly report of CBW field team chief," in CBW Box 1 (Cables, Southeast Asia), National Security Archive.

An article in the *New York Times* by Philip M. Boffey, dated August 31, 1987, "Washington Talk: Chemical Warfare; Declassified Cables Add to Doubts about US Disclosures on 'Yellow Rain.'"

Articles in the *New Yorker* by Thomas Whiteside, dated February 11, 1991, "Annals of the Cold War: The Yellow-Rain Complex—I," and February 18, 1991, "Annals of the Cold War: The Yellow-Rain Complex—II."

Rebecca Katz's 2005 PhD dissertation, *Yellow Rain Revisited: Lessons Learned for the Investigation of Chemical and Biological Weapons Allegations*, completed at Princeton University, UMI Number: 3161973.

"Burn Copies"

The information and graphics for this piece were drawn and excerpted from:

A cover letter, dated September 24, 1971, from George A. Carver, Jr., Special Assistant for Vietnamese Affairs to Mr. Dan Arnold. Declassified August 12, 2005, document number: CIA-RDP80R01720R000700020042-3. CREST, General CIA records. Published on Central Intelligence Agency FOIA (http://www.foia.cia.gov).

Daniel Arnold served as CIA Chief of Station (COS) in Vientiane starting in 1973 and was the last COS to serve in this position before Laos fell to the communists.

"Diary Notes from Meeting on September 13, 1983"

This poem's epigraph and italicized areas were excerpted from:
> A declassified cable, dated October 31, 1983, from the US Embassy in Bangkok to the Secretary of State in Washington, DC, subject heading: "Reports of LPDR crackdown on Hmong," in CBW Box 1 (Cables, Southeast Asia and Afghanistan), National Security Archive.

"For as Long as a Mountain Can Ascend"

The information for this poem and its epigraph were drawn from:
> A declassified cable, dated October 12, 1978, from the US Embassy in Bangkok to the Secretary of State in Washington, DC, subject heading: "Hmong refugee stories," in CBW Box 5 (Cables 1978–1987), National Security Archive.

> A declassified cable, dated November 3, 1978, from the US Embassy in Bangkok to the Secretary of State in Washington, DC, subject heading unknown, in CBW Box 5 (Cables 1978–1987), National Security Archive.

The watermark graphic was pulled from:
> A declassified cable, dated April 19, 1985, from the US Embassy in Bangkok to the Secretary of State in Washington, DC, subject heading: "Ninth quarterly report of CBW field team chief," in CBW Box 1 (Cables, Southeast Asia), National Security Archive.

"Subject: ROI"

This poem's epigraph was excerpted from:
> A memorandum of conversation, dated August 5, 1970, participants included Ambassador G. McMurtrie Godley, US Ambassador to Laos, Dr. Henry A. Kissinger, Mr. John J. Holdridge, time and place: Dr. Kissinger's office on July 23, 1970, on the subject of: "Ambassador Godley's comments on developments in Laos." Declassified January 1, 2015, document number: LOC-HAK-508-2-11-3. CREST, Collection: Library of Congress. Published on Central Intelligence Agency FOIA (http://www.foia.cia.gov).

The watermark graphic was pulled from:
> A declassified cable, date unknown, routing unknown, subject heading unknown, in CBW Box 1 (Cables, Southeast Asia), National Security Archive.

"How Far for the Small Ones"

The italicized areas in this poem were excerpted from:
> A declassified cable, dated October 16, 1981, from the US Embassy in Bangkok to the Secretary of State in Washington, DC, subject heading unknown, in CBW Box 5 (Cables 1978–1987), National Security Archive.

A report, dated January 18, 1983, subject heading: "Ban Vinai Camp." Declassified by DIA April 24, 2003, declassification #153264, Armed Forces Medical Intelligence Center.

A declassified cable, dated October 28, 1983, from the US Embassy in Bangkok to the Secretary of State in Washington, DC, subject heading: "Hmong CBW sample," in CBW Box 1 (Cables, Southeast Asia and Afghanistan), National Security Archive.

"Monument"

This poem is for the late Hmong poet Pos Moua. In memoriam.

"Manifesto of a Drum"

The eagle watermark graphic was pulled from:

A fax cover sheet, dated April 22, 1982, from the United States Army Medical Intelligence and Information Agency (USAMIIA) to the United States Army Foreign Science and Technology Center (FSTC), subject heading unknown. Declassified by DIA October 9, 2003, declassification #152511, Armed Forces Medical Intelligence Center.

Acknowledgments

Grateful to the editors at the following publications where versions of these poems first appeared:

The American Poetry Review: "Refugee, Walking Is the Most Human of All," "The Shaman Asks about Yellow Rain"

Catamaran Literary Reader: "Revolt of Bees"

Freeman's: "Prayer to the Redwood"

Guernica: "Subterfuge"

Los Angeles Review of Books: "And Yet Still More"

NECK: "Noxious," "Signal for the Way Out"

Poetry: "For the Nefarious," "Monument"

The Rumpus: "Sorrowed"

The Scores: "Allied with the Bees," "A Daub of Tree Swallows as Aerial Ash,"

Tin House: "Authorization to Depart Ravaged Homeland as Biomedical Sample"

West Branch: "Declassified," "Vigil for the Missing"

Women's Studies Quarterly: "They Think Our Killed Ones Cannot Speak to Us," "Anthem for Taking Back"

I owe a great deal of thanks to Dr. Rebecca Katz whose dissertation and work on yellow rain were invaluable to my research. Thank you also to *Politics and the Life Sciences* as well as the National Security Archive at George Washington University for providing me with access to their declassified files.

For gifting me with time, space, and resources to carry out this work, I wish to thank the Lannan Foundation and its residency program in Marfa, the Jeannette Haien Ballard Prize, and Civitella Ranieri. Many thanks also to Jessica Strand.

For the professional support to undertake this work, gratitude goes to the MFA Writing Program at the School of the Art Institute of Chicago (SAIC) and the MFA Program in Creative Writing at Fresno State. Thank you also to my colleagues in the English Department at Fresno State.

To the extraordinary team at Graywolf Press, and to Jeff Shotts, Chantz Erolin, and Katie Dublinski for the editorial care, vision, and support. I'm incredibly appreciative!

To Don Mee Choi, Tyehimba Jess, Viet Thanh Nguyen, and Kao Kalia Yang, for your generous words in support of this work, I offer my gratitude.

Many thanks to those who have helped along the way: Kaveh Akbar, CAConrad, Eduardo Corral, Carolina Ebeid, Carolyn Forché, Juan Felipe Herrera, Ilya Kaminsky, Nam Le, Dr. Aline Lo, Dr. Louisa Schein, Ying Thao, Burlee Vang, Soul Vang, Ocean Vuong, Khaty Xiong, Andre Yang, Lar Yang, MaiKa Yang, and my students at Fresno State.

For community, with thanks to the Hmong American Writers' Circle, Hmong American Ink and Stories, Kundiman, and the Laureate Lab Visual Wordist Studio at Fresno State.

To my family, thank you for the encouragement. And to Anthony Cody who helped me sift through countless pages of archival material during the initial research phase, grateful for your love, patience, and support.

Always, for remembrance.

Mai Der Vang is the author of *Afterland,* winner of the Walt Whitman Award of the Academy of American Poets, longlisted for the National Book Award in Poetry, and a finalist for the Kate Tufts Discovery Award. The recipient of a Lannan Literary Fellowship, she served as a visiting writer at the School of the Art Institute of Chicago. Vang earned degrees from the University of California, Berkeley, and Columbia University. She teaches in the MFA Program in Creative Writing at Fresno State.

This book is made possible through a partnership with the College of Saint Benedict, and honors the legacy of S. Mariella Gable, a distinguished teacher at the College.

Previous titles in this series include:

Support for this series has been provided by the Manitou Fund as part of the Warner Reading Program.

The text of *Yellow Rain* is set in Warnock Pro.
Book design by Rachel Holscher.
Composition by Bookmobile Design & Digital
Publisher Services, Minneapolis, Minnesota.
Manufactured by McNaughton & Gunn on acid-free,
100 percent postconsumer wastepaper.